CENTER

OF THE

UNIVERSE

TOO

DESTINY IMAGE BOOKS BY BILL JOHNSON

A Life of Miracles

Dreaming With God

Release the Power of Jesus

Strengthen Yourself in the Lord

The Supernatural Power of a Transformed Mind

When Heaven Invades Earth

Here Comes Heaven

Spiritual Java

Center of the Universe

Momentum

Walking in the Supernatural

Hosting the Presence

BILL JOHNSON

CENTER
OF THE
UNIVERSE
TOO

*A Look at Life
from the Lighter Side*

DESTINY IMAGE® PUBLISHERS, INC.
P.O. Box 310, Shippensburg, PA 17257-0310
"Promoting Inspired Lives."

This book and all other Destiny Image, Revival Press, MercyPlace, Fresh Bread, Destiny Image Fiction, and Treasure House books are available at Christian bookstores and distributors worldwide.

For a U.S. bookstore nearest you, call 1-800-722-6774.
For more information on foreign distributors, call 717-532-3040.
Reach us on the Internet: www.destinyimage.com.

ISBN 13 TP: 978-0-7684-0325-1
ISBN 13 Ebook: 978-0-7684-8575-2

For Worldwide Distribution, Printed in the U.S.A.

1 2 3 4 5 6 7 8 / 17 16 15 14 13

Contents

1

COUNSELING

While I'm not a great counselor, I have learned that anyone who knows a bit of the Bible and loves people can learn to help others. Counseling is a ministry that has come into prominence in recent years, sometimes for the wrong reasons, but still, it's one worthy of our respect. Counsel is elevated in the Bible by Solomon, who teaches its importance for anyone interested in a life of wisdom. We are commanded to seek it before making important decisions. (See Proverbs 1:5; 11:14; 19:21 and others.)

Years ago I worked in a youth ministry called the Salt House. In our work with young people we emphasized discipleship, and in turn led these disciples in evangelism. Much of our time was spent in counseling. At least two of our workers went on to become professionals in that field.

Much of our evangelistic work was with drug addicts and users. Because of this kind of focus, two nursing students from Chico State University came to interview me as part of a class project. Their report was on the services that were provided for the young people with drug problems. They decided to use our ministry as a resource.

To say that they were skeptical about our untrained staff is like saying that sumo wrestlers are simply larger than average men. Everything about my interview told me I was on trial. Here I was, 20 years old, trying to help people who the professionals were unable to help. I could understand their disbelief. It was a bit overwhelming for me too. During our interview they learned that we had a board of directors—men of distinction both in the church and in their professions—who helped oversee our ministry. Of the six members, one was a medical doctor and another was a psychiatrist. With that information, I finally seemed to have a moment of favor with the students...that is until they asked me if I sent referrals to the psychiatrist (all the people we had no business trying to help). Before thinking, I said, "We've never sent anyone to him, but he has sent some to us." I fell out of favor quickly. I love how God works, using the foolish things to confound the wise.

Through the years I have learned a couple of things about people coming for counsel: they seldom lie, and they seldom tell the truth. Let me explain.

People usually say things that are true, but seldom say all that needs to be said in order to identify the real problem. A wife may say, "My husband left home last night, and hasn't called me to let me know where he is." It's a rare person who will make up a story like that. But, what she may neglect to tell me is that she threw a vase at him and told him not to come back, ever. While she didn't lie, neither did she tell the truth.

A counselor is like a teacher in that they are to communicate truth to people. Often when I speak to hungry Bible school students, I find myself speaking in an authority that is greater than my norm. Hunger brings it out. God is so committed to feeding the spiritually hungry, that we (teachers) end up speaking of things that we never before understood until that meeting. It is the same for the counselor; he or she speaks with a power that is either enhanced or hindered by the honesty and hunger of the one seeking help.

What is it to be honest? It starts with being truthful to ourselves. Once we've done that, we must carry it to its logical conclusion and confess to God. It'll never catch Him off guard. Some fear His rejection. Yet God never rejects the humble, only the proud.

One of the greatest signs of spiritual pride is the inability to confess sin, whether in attitude, thought, or action. Parents, or others in authority, often avoid confession, fearing that it weakens their position before the ones they serve. The opposite is true. Parents who refuse to confess sin to their children will find that a communication gap grows as the kids become older. Why? Because children are very aware of their parents' weaknesses. While they don't require perfection, they do require honesty. To refuse to acknowledge sin can be a form of dishonesty. And good communication is built on trust, which has truthfulness as its foundation.

The pathway to success, according to Scripture, is very simple. Do things God's way. Part of our success in life is measured by friendships—people who are loyal, devoted to God, and will offer help and support as is needed. At times we must seek out the specialist for help or counsel. But most of the time, a friend who loves God and will be honest with us will do just fine. Paul, in referring to how the Body functions said, *"...speaking the truth in love"* (Eph. 4:15). Truth and love are the work of the counselor and the average Christian alike. And so, encourage and be encouraged. Take full advantage of the counseling ministry that takes place every day in our lives with committed believers. That is the normal Christian life.

2

HAIRCUTS

I cried after a bad haircut once. I was in the 9th grade. The barber, apparently just released from the military for cutting young recruits' hair too short, approached my head with a sense of mission. I cried with embarrassment and anger. It only takes one bad haircut to make you a nerd. It seemed to me that such a person shouldn't be allowed to live, at least not within a hundred yards of a pair of scissors.

I never did like haircuts. They take way too much time. Even though short hair has been "in" for years, I struggle with it. I have always liked my hair to be a little longer than normal. Well, almost always.

Like many young boys, I had a crew cut while growing up. In fact, that was the only period of time that I enjoyed doing the barber routine. And it wasn't because I actually liked short hair. Dad would drive me to downtown Sacramento and drop me off at the barbershop. I then had the honor of taking the 10-cent bus ride home by myself.

Riding the bus was a treat, but the real fun was a window seat and a peashooter. I would buy one at the neighborhood market before boarding the bus. There were so many unsuspecting drivers with their windows down stopped at red lights, so many bored pedestrians, all needing a *wake me up* experience. And I was their gift. Since it was a rather mischievous activity, it was one I had to enjoy by myself; and I quietly laughed at my successes.

Soon after the bus-riding era ended, the Beatles arrived on the scene. Their hair length inspired a departure from the crew cut norm. I, for one, was glad to see the change; I think that the butch wax I used might have caused some minor brain damage.

I gradually grew my hair to new socially acceptable lengths. In the midst of my newfound liberty, our high school football team decided that to display solidarity and discipline we should require all team members to get a butch. Four of us went to the local barbershop together to give him the shearing privileges. After he finished, he lined us up and gave his opinion on our looks. To the first he said, "You don't look too bad. And neither do you," he said to the second.

The barber stopped when he came to me and said, "But don't you ever get your hair cut like this again!" My feelings exactly.

I am blessed. Not only does my wife cut my hair my way, she does so patiently. Her patience is needed because I am picky. Plus, being still has never been my strong suit. It's not that I am hyperactive. I just don't like sitting still for a long period of time. (It must be related to the times when I had to sit still to have my picture taken; my eyes would go dry and they needed a thousand blinks to clear them. And then there would be itches in places that hadn't itched for years, all while the camera was clicking. I think it's an allergic reaction to *stillness*.) My wife has also displayed her patience by cutting my hair the same way for the past many years. Her sense of adventure would have me in different styles every other month, and who knows, maybe even different colors! But she just smiles, and cuts.

Some who have the Stillness Allergy find that they always have to be working. They get home from the job and continue working by doing things around the house until bedtime. My disease is not of that particular strain. I just don't want to be still. If I'm watching a movie, I'll usually have a magazine or a book in my lap to keep me busy. Even my prayer time is often combined with walking.

God is patient too, just like my wife (actually, I think she got it from Him). He constantly puts me in situations to teach me one simple lesson—how to sit still. In His Word He puts it like this, *"Be still, and know that I am God"* (Ps. 46:10). When I obey, I discover Him. Wow! The word *still* means to *let go*. That seems appropriate. For me to be still usually means I have to let go of something. Sometimes it's worries and cares, sometimes it's my own agenda, and occasionally it's even my ideas of what He is like. God often speaks with "the still small voice" mentioned in Scripture. That is to remind us that it is in the stillness that we hear His voice the best. And as I learn the value of stillness, I am finding a world of opportunities in which to grow.

Isn't this strange? I don't like to sit still, but I love stillness, after I've let go and actually done things His way. He knows what I need. But that doesn't mean I'll ever like haircuts.

3

IF IT TASTES GOOD

I actually enjoy health foods. You know, the kind that has texture similar to cardboard and other fibrous materials. This week I bought a couple of healthy muffins. During the eating process, I discovered that some building materials were actually developed in the kitchen—particleboard to be more specific. These muffins actually had character. What they lacked in flavor, they made up for in...well, in being conversation pieces. And just to prove that I really enjoy health food, I went in and bought another one today—from the same batch. As they always say, "The only thing worse than a health food muffin is an old health food muffin." And if that's not something they always say, remember, you heard it here first.

These statements are usually true: "If it tastes good, it must be bad for you." Or worse yet, "If it's dry and tasteless, it must be good for you."

The view that bad-for-you foods taste good has affected more than just our diets. The church has for a long time thought that if there is pleasure in it then it must not be from God. He is seen as the Great Mercy Giver, that is, until you're saved. And once you're in the family, watch out! Remember well that first joy, because that's the last you may see of it. I've never heard anyone say that, yet its followers are easy to spot.

When I was growing up, I figured that we were stuck with music that related better to an older generation. Contemporary church music was actually gospel quartets—while enjoyed by many, it's not exactly my idea of something that reflected the present youth culture. But that was all we had until the late '60s. The Jesus Movement swept the country, as well as many nations of the world. It's hard not to sing about Jesus when you've met Him. And that generation began to do it the only way they knew how, with the style they knew how to play.

It would have been tragic if they had tried to conform to the existing church traditions. All we would have had is more of what we already had. God's work is fresh and new. He always relates well to every generation and culture. It's hard to be more *now* than He who is the great *I Am.* Of course, there are always those who criticize God's present work, especially if He didn't start with them, or do it to their liking. But that's another issue for another day.

A young man from another time once asked his dad, "Why does the devil have all the good music?" His father replied, "If you think you can do better, write some of your own." He did. His name was Isaac Watts. He is recognized as one of the greatest hymn writers in all of Church history. Of course, in his day they were considered very contemporary tunes. He was a good communicator in that he delivered an uncompromising message in a way that best suited his audience.

Bach, considered by many to be the greatest musician of all time, was a very devoted Christian. (Why is it necessary to classify some Christians as "very devoted"?) He was fired from at least one job as church organist because he was too contemporary. Today he is old-fashioned (but a personal favorite).

Why do we tend to value the prophet after he is dead and gone? If he's dead, he's revered. If he's alive and unique or challenging, many complain.

Why does the Church approve the world's standards in a previous generation, after it's no longer in style? What makes that style less holy now that it's not popular? Is it the fact that it is liked by unbelievers that makes something unholy?

Why do we so often settle for second best in the name of humility? Or worse yet, live in mediocrity because we believe that if it tastes bad it must be good for us? Is it the person who only knows prayer and study who best reflects the nature of God? Or could it be the one who also enjoys flowers and music, or mountains and rivers, or even a good movie, along with the obviously spiritual elements of life?

I'm not sure of all the answers. I only know of my own determination—I want to delight in God to the maximum, to where that joy infects every aspect of my life. I also want to relate this boundless joy to a world that would do anything for just a taste. They have a right to know that this God we serve, the Great Mercy Giver, has mercy that is new every morning. And this must be evident in our zest for life.

You know what's scary? You can acquire a taste for muffins with the texture of cardboard and rice cakes that are strangely akin to Styrofoam. I know this from experience. But I'm also glad that when the psalmist said, *"Taste and see that the Lord is good"* (Ps. 34:8), he knew that knowing Jesus is not an acquired taste. He is what our hearts have cried out for since birth. Finally, something that tastes good is good for you.

4

JERKING

One Tuesday night I had the chance to minister to a number of people in our renewal meetings. God's power was so strong. I felt that God showed me that He would give some of them a special opportunity to meet with Him, saying, "And it may be at three o'clock in the morning. Be ready. You'll know it's Him." Little did I know what God had in store *for me.*

Following that meeting, Beni and I finally got to bed around 1 A.M. I was awakened suddenly by the presence of God and my shaking body. I glanced at the clock and it was 3 A.M. exactly, and I realized that the prophecy was also for me. From 3 until 6:38 A.M. when I got up, my body shook uncontrollably. Why? I don't know. But it felt like God took my finger and stuck it in His electrical socket. I was experiencing a heavenly power surge.

Throughout that next day I was unusually aware of God's presence, with a subtle trembling inside. The next night was even stranger. The presence of God was strong. His holiness has a way of becoming known. My body shook again; this time from the moment I went to bed until I got up the next morning. I had no control. I thought that maybe if I could relax enough I could override this phenomenon. What a stupid thought—override God. I could relax for about 15 seconds. Then suddenly, my body would erupt as though an internal bomb had gone off—my arms and legs jerking about in a most embarrassing way. There was a time when, if I had seen someone with such a manifestation, I would have tried to cast out the devil. But the peace of God was simply overwhelming.

Beni and I must have looked like two folks ready for men in white coats to come after us. Picture this: I'm lying there giving new meaning to the term *jerk*, and she's laughing uncontrollably. Brian comes into the room and can hardly believe that his normally reserved dad is bouncing around the waterbed in such a strange way, and his mom is hysterical. He runs to wake his sister Leah saying, "Come and see what Mom and Dad are doing in bed!" Steve Martin couldn't create a funnier scene with better lines. God wouldn't let go of me—but I didn't want Him to.

Imagine my concern. The next morning I had an orthodontist appointment. This *jerking thing* hits especially hard when I'm lying down. The orthodontist chair puts me in that position. How do I explain flailing arms and legs to a room full of professionals? While the jerks I actually experienced in the chair weren't violent, they were there. Thankfully I was able to camouflage them quite well. No explaining was necessary.

Last night was the same. God was there; and I shook uncontrollably all night long. With very little sleep, I got up again today fully refreshed and ready to go. Even Beni slept well in the turbulent sea of our waterbed. It's unexplainable.

Perhaps the funniest part of all is that I have had this happen many times in recent years, but was unaware of the source. While it never lasted all night, it would take place for maybe up to an hour. My only thought was that I must have eaten poorly that day, and that my muscles were reacting to a lack of who knows what. I feel somewhat like Samuel who heard his name called several times, but didn't realize that it was God who was doing the calling.

What is the fruit of all this? One: care-less-ness. I care less about things that have eaten away at my time, and more importantly, my affections. Two: my awareness of God's presence has increased dramatically. Three: my hunger for God is stronger by the day. All I want to do is pray, worship, talk about Him, and minister in His power. Four: it's not over, and some fruit takes awhile to grow.

Is this jerking stuff confusing? Yes. My head doesn't have a clue what's going on. I have tried to analyze this movement, but have not come up with many profound answers. However, Apostle Paul taught us that, *"The natural man does not receive the things of the Spirit of God, for they are foolishness to him; nor can he know them, because they are spiritually discerned"* (1 Cor. 2:14). But my heart is pretty thrilled...enough to make up for what my head lacks.

How can anybody in their right mind jerk about like a mental case, all the while asking God for more? A week ago that might have seemed foolish to me. But last night I cried throughout the night, "More God, more!"

5

RECEIVING CORRECTION

While attending Genesis Discipleship Training Center, I worked as a Custodial Engineer (janitor). My responsibilities were to bring about environmental changes (clean) within the Santa Rosa City Hall and the Police Department. It was a fascinating job, one for which I had been well-groomed. I had worked for the Redding School District the previous year in the same profession.

One evening I started talking about the weather with a city official who was working late. In describing something, he used the name "Jesus Christ," except he wasn't talking to or about Him. So I mentioned that if he only knew Him, he wouldn't use the Name like that. Oops…the guy wasn't interested in being corrected by anyone, especially one who takes out his trash. He began to tell me in a somewhat louder tone that I didn't have the right to preach to him like that. I thought to myself, *That was a sermon?* It's the shortest sermon I'll ever give.

My next project was the Police Department. While I was working, the dispatcher started a short conversation between calls. He also used the Name, even though Jesus wasn't the subject. Still recovering from my last "alien" encounter, I mentioned that he wouldn't talk like that if he only knew Him. His response was totally different. He apologized for his insensitivity. And I forgave him.

People's responses to correction are interesting. Some welcome it. Others become rigid, glaring at you as though their eyes came equipped with laser guns. And still others let us know what we can do with our nugget of truth. And quite honestly, that variety of responses exists within the Church too.

I have a love-hate relationship with correction. I love it because the Bible tells me to, and because it brings me closer to my life's goal—to be like Jesus. I hate it because "Who does he think he is?" and because it hurts. But when all is said and done, I discover that all that was hurt was pride, which Jesus is determined to kill anyway.

Sometimes the hardest people to receive correction from are those closest to you. For that reason my wife and I have given each other an invitation to address anything that we might see in the other that needs changing. It is an invitation we have used, without wearing out our welcome.

Try it. You'll hate it. But in the end, you'll love it. I promise.

6

TELEVISION

I love to have control of the remote control for our TV. In our house it's called *the mantle*. Since we have a satellite dish, we can scan more of the things that aren't worth watching than those who simply have cable.

Sometimes, when I come home after a Friday night prayer meeting, I sit down in front of the tube for just a moment before retiring. It's hard for me to go right to bed. I turn on the television to see if there is anything to watch. I usually go to bed after an honest effort of channel surfing, having come up empty more than once.

It's no secret that men watch television differently from women. Women have been known to turn to a particular channel because there will be a program on in an hour that they want to watch. A man, on the other hand, will even scan other channels during the commercials of the program he is watching—except for the Super Bowl, when the commercials are usually better than the game.

Such strenuous scanning can be taxing on the brain. In order to regain a little of my lost sanity (and to get rid of my guilt for controlling the TV), I surrender the *mantle* to my wife, usually with the kids protesting. She turns to one of the classic movie channels for a good old black and white, or maybe even a corny, slightly more modern movie with color. We have been known to groan and travail when it looks as though we might be locked into an Oldie but Goodie. It seldom helps.

Advertisers are not only aware of the phenomenon of men and women and their remote; they mock us. Notice that I said *us* (men). The woman who is willing to wait for an hour because something *will be* on is not mocked. No. It is we who travel at high speeds over the original information highway that are taunted.

Family sitcoms have enjoyed playing off the difference of the sexes for years. Cosby himself has smiled all the way to the bank with his great family show. That was one I could watch without fear that something weird was about to happen. *Home Improvement* now holds the torch for family comedy. These shows are very enjoyable and seem to be growing in number. But is there one where the father or husband is not the brunt of the joke? (Allow me just a moment to have an overly sensitive male reaction, please.)

What would the outcry be if the wife were the one who constantly had the wrong counsel for their children? What if she were the one who had no clue about how to deal with the relatives, or their finances, etc.? Or what about the commercials? Two men are arguing in the back seat of the taxi because they are stuck in traffic and are going to be late to a meeting. They are frustrated and confused, until the woman in the front seat quietly takes over the situation (in a Clint Eastwood fashion) by hooking up the computer to her cellular phone and faxing their proposal to the appropriate location. Is this an accurate display of the business community? Perhaps occasionally. But only occasionally.

Are there commercials where the husband and father have the answers to the family's dilemmas? Isn't it usually the wife, or even the children who teach the dad?

Or what about politicians? When was the last time one was shown as a person of integrity or as one who really cares about the people he or she serves? Or when was the last time you saw a movie about a person who owned a large business that was not portrayed as an uncaring, uncompassionate crook? And God forbid that this businessman is actually a CEO of a corporation of IBM-like proportions. They are seldom (*never* might be more accurate) portrayed as people of character.

These generalizations on TV are inaccurate and unfortunate. The young accountant will bring down the corporate president because it helps to sell tickets in the theater. If the father had all the answers for the family (circa "Father Knows Best"—equally untrue) few people would watch. They have done a great job of grabbing our interest with humorous themes. I enjoy their story lines, but…

Have you watched an old movie with surprise and wonder at how they got away with the obvious bigotry toward blacks and other minorities? The blatant put-down of women was common and stupid. The generalizations of a previous generation were cruel, but socially acceptable by the majority. What is being mocked today that we'll regret tomorrow? Much, including the Christian.

The citizens of the Kingdom of God live by a different code of ethics. This code doesn't change with the times. The fact that it's now the 21st century means nothing to the one who is devoted to the One Who Changes Not! Our culture is the culture of Heaven. In this culture no one is rejected; all are loved. No one is mocked; everyone is encouraged. No one is belittled; everyone is served.

Does that mean that I can't watch *Cosby* at work? No. Not at all. Many of these shows are well written and are very entertaining. I have even enjoyed the commercials that I've mentioned. The writers have touched on a subject that helps us remember their product—and that is successful advertising. Just enjoy them for what they are. Know the difference between the real and the unreal. And know the Kingdom's never-changing culture. Like God Himself, it is eternal.

7

WHAT TO WEAR?

A fellow pastor and I drove all night to attend Jack Hayford's Pastors' Conference. We felt like we were going to Mecca. The year was 1974.

Our pseudo-hippie appearance was enhanced by having been up all night. The shoulder-length hair, Levi jeans, tee shirts and tennis shoes all spoke of the part of our culture that we represented. And it apparently spoke rather loudly.

When we arrived at the church they were still setting up for the conference that was to start that evening. The registration tables were in place, and the workers were preparing for the influx of several hundred pastors. As we stood there, watching the workers quickly moving about, no one came to assist us. After a good amount of time had passed, a woman stopped to find out why we were just standing there. When we told her we were there for the conference, she asked us if we had come to help in the kitchen.

After recovering from a hearty laugh, we revealed our secret identity—we were pastors. Her mistake didn't bother us. We probably deserved it. But she felt badly. She personally registered us for the week and set up our housing. At that time they put up all the visiting pastors in the homes of the people who were members of the church. When she called the folks we were to stay with, she explained that we were "their kind of people," and that when we arrived at their home, they shouldn't think they were about to be mugged. I didn't think we looked *that* bad.

Appearance was a big issue as a young person. I grew up in a generation whose goal was to be nonconformists. And so we all dressed the same, in a nonconforming way. We felt free, no longer encumbered by the traditions of our forefathers, especially the need to wear a coat and tie or dress, etc. And then God started meddling. It's amazing how spiritually right our own culture seems to be, and how hard it is to change to His culture. After all, we would exclaim, *"for man looks on the outward appearance, but the Lord looks at the heart"* (1 Sam. 16:7). Have you ever quoted Scriptures to God, trying to help Him better understand what He said and why? Don't bother.

A fellow minister once tried to help me by addressing what he felt was a lack of excellence in the way I dressed. I told him that in my community suits and ties were rare at best. He responded with a good point: as the pastor, I am the one who sets the standard, and people will follow me. I took his counsel to heart. And he was right. Men started wearing coats and ties. Forget the fact that no one was allowed to minister from the platform unless they wore what I considered to be excellent. I guess that's one way to get people to follow. Make 'em hungry to serve, and then let them do so until they dress right. I had finally settled the clothing issue, and was able to do the suit and tie thing.

In 1987, I, along with several of our church leaders, attended a Signs and Wonders Conference with John Wimber in Anaheim, California. He is another great man of God, one from whom I'd like to have a whole lot more of God rub off on me. This conference had a couple of thousand people in attendance. Imagine this—the men from the small mountain community, looking very spiritual and pastoral. Our ties were colorful and the white shirts were neatly pressed. The sport jacket I was wearing complemented my slacks, giving me that contemporary look without appearing stuffy. I left the three-piece suit at home. My hair was neatly trimmed and godly looking.

There was one problem. The seven of us were probably the only ones in the place who appeared so godly. We actually looked like the Charismatic Mafia. All we needed were violin cases to put our big black Bibles in. And by golly, we weren't going to allow those poor souls with low standards in excellence to affect those of us who had set our sights on loftier things. And so, day after day, session after session, we sat looking good, with 2,000 other people who looked like the kitchen help.

This conflict in dress may seem like a simple thing to you, but it's been traumatic for me. I'd like to know just what God wants. Is it ties or Levi's? I'm a pastor. I should know this kind of thing. And it's challenging questions like this that urge me on to greater study.

I got my concordance out and looked up the word *clothing*. Perhaps there would be an answer for this important issue that I had overlooked in my years of study. I found many interesting verses. One such verse talked about Jesus' clothing after His resurrection. It was pretty bright stuff. Another talked of how the soldiers gambled for His clothing at His crucifixion. But neither of those applied. And then I ran across Matthew 6:28, which says, *"So why do you worry about clothing?"* That seemed like a fitting question to me. I couldn't figure out why I was so anxious. And then it hit me. A verse that I had overlooked answers all my questions about my attire. *"Put on the Lord Jesus Christ"* (Rom. 13:14). That's it! I have found what satisfies my heart.

What about suits and ties? Don't worry about it. Wear what you enjoy. But be sure to put on Jesus! After all, it's only the Pharisees who think you have to dress like them to be really spiritual. And they're a tough group to please. Just ask Jesus.

8

TESTING GOD

The daydreams of a child are usually filled with flight—from room to room, throughout the neighborhoods, in and around school, all without effort or danger. I don't ever remember wanting to fly like a bird. The continual flapping of their wings looked rather exhausting to me. I preferred to fly more like Superman. And since it was my daydream, I could fly any way I wanted. That is, until I woke up from this dream and had to walk home from school.

At the age of 5 I became fascinated with parachutes. One day at school we took paper napkins and tied strings to the four corners. At the end of the strings we tied a little plastic army man. It was great to throw this toy into the air and watch the little guy float down to earth without harm. This experience brought flying within reach for me.

I got home and climbed a tree with my army man in hand. Tied to him was the parachute that I had already tested. I was sure it worked. After all, my plastic soldier floated safely to earth. So I climbed as high as I dared, untangled the strings of the parachute, held on to the plastic man, and jumped.

Sometimes we learn from books. And sometimes we learn from experience. In that, my first flight, I received a revelation somewhere between *terra firma* and the limb of the tree. I don't know the name of the law that would describe the lesson for the day—experience doesn't always provide us with the proper titles. But it had something to do with the size of the parachute correlating to the size of the soldier. Needless to say I met Planet Earth that day in a way I shall always remember.

God made laws that govern our lives. There are natural laws, and there are spiritual laws. I can scream all I want about God and His unjust law of gravity. Yet, He is neither intimidated nor impressed by my reactions. And the law works with or without my approval.

Some have chosen to test God, to go against the laws that He has made hoping that God will intervene and spare them of their deserved rewards. Some intentionally drink poison and handle rattlesnakes. (I wouldn't be a very good member of that group. I don't even take to snakes in *National Geographic*.)

Others buy big screen TVs without money, hoping for God to supply when the payment is due.

Jesus, the only One with the position and understanding to test His heavenly Father, knew it was a violation of their relationship. He resisted such an opportunity by refusing to jump from the pinnacle of the temple to prove to Satan that the Father would protect Him (see Luke 4:9-12).

Testing God is forbidden in Scripture. It is manipulative and therefore borders on cultic activity. But surprisingly, God gave one exception to this awesome law. And in this exception He not only allows us to bring Him to the test, He commands us to do so. The area is the tithe—10 percent of your income given to the local church for the work of the ministry—and offerings. He did so by saying, "'...And try Me now in this,' says the Lord of hosts, 'If I will not open for you the windows of heaven and pour out for you such blessing that there will not be room enough to receive it'" (Mal. 3:10).

Imagine the Awesome God being tested. I doubt that the angels, who behold His face every day, could ever comprehend how God would command us to bring Him to a test. He obviously desires to reveal His character to humankind in a way we would never forget. It's a command of love and mercy.

If you haven't done so already, accept His invitation to be part of the miracle, the ongoing support of the Gospel in the earth, and a supernatural invasion of your finances. Give back what already belongs to Him, the tithe. Consider it rent. It's His planet you're living on.

9

RESTITUTION

As a pastor, I have often had to wrestle with some questions that arise as I observe people's lives unfolding according to the choices they make. How is it that one young person who has confessed Christ ends up a drug addict, denying the Gospel? And how does one raised in a hellish home live faithfully for God throughout his life? I've concluded that your family of origin is not what determines who you will be, though it has a big influence on the choices you will make. A good family upbringing is like a full bank account. It means you may start out ahead of others, but it's no guarantee of where you'll end up. It depends on what you do with what you have.

In looking back to my youth, I remember many young people who experienced renewal in Christ. The Jesus Movement of the early '70s was an amazing thing to witness. Hundreds of thousands, if not millions, confessed Christ. Some have endured the difficulties of the following years and continue to enjoy the faithfulness of our God. Others...

In the epistles, we can see that Paul experienced this frustration as he poured out his life in the ministry of the Gospel. Some of his spiritual sons would become distracted by the world and its provisions, and lose the heart to give all. (Giving all is the only safe way to walk with God. Anything short of that is too dangerous for my liking.) Others, in the midst of circumstances that would crush many, seemed to flourish. Why?

While there may be various reasons for why people fall away from the Lord, I believe that those who stick with it have embraced a practical expression of their faith called *restitution*. Restitution is God's way of enabling us to make a break with our past. A fresh beginning is what God has promised to all who come to Him. But it is vital to realize that this beginning is only the first part of the journey—a journey that will be continually characterized by the process of letting old values and behaviors go in order to replace them with those of the Kingdom. Restitution means to *restore, renew*, or *repay*. If I have stolen, I make restitution by confessing my sin and paying back the debt.

During my high school days, I lived with my football coach for part of my senior year. One day while cleaning out the '57 Chevy he just bought, I found a transistor radio. I picked it up and used it. When I moved, I took it with me. Several years later I became aware of that sin. I hadn't planned to steal it, but I was careless with what belonged to another. When the Holy Spirit turned on His spotlight, I saw that underneath my carelessness was a heart of greed. That carelessness led me to do what I never considered myself to be capable of—stealing. I confessed it, not as a mistake or error in judgment, but as sin. It became necessary to write to my coach, who lived at the other end of the state, and apologize, enclosing a check to cover the cost of what I had taken.

For people who have lived a life of crime, it may appear impossible to make restitution for every wrong they have done. The truth is that none of us have the ability to make up for the grief or loss that our sin may have caused. If we could, we wouldn't need the Cross. God invites us to partner daily with Him in walking out our repentance and burning the bridges to our past so that our enemy cannot convince us that we aren't the people God loves with all His heart.

Here are some things to remember as you face issues that require restitution in your life. First of all, nothing is impossible. Second, the Holy Spirit knows what needs to be done and what doesn't. Ask Him. He loves to talk to you. Third, it's important to remember that restitution is not about *earning forgiveness*. It is simply putting repentance into practice. Zacchaeus, *that wee little man*, knew this principle well. He said, *"If I have taken anything from anyone by false accusation, I restore fourfold"* (Luke 19:8). Was he commanded to do that? No. It was the evidence of real faith—real repentance.

Restitution doesn't always involve material things. In fact, the most often used expression of restitution is seen in *confession*. It's the simple act of going to another person, taking responsibility for our words or actions, and giving a full apology, asking for forgiveness. This brings us to the place of *humility*, that underrated world of faith, love, and power. Considering that *pride* is the root of all sin, it would make sense that anytime we humble ourselves we distance our hearts from the affections of this world. Worldliness and humility are worlds apart. It's difficult to walk in humility and have any kind of desire to return to sin. Difficult? No, impossible!

Of all the Christians we've known over the years, those who have practiced this simple principle, confessing their sin to their brothers and sisters, are those who walk in power and confidence today. The world has lost its appeal, and the values of the Kingdom become more and more entrenched as their personal way of life. The tragedy is that this life was promised to all who believe. And so few enter in—really enter in.

It is amazing to me how few people are able to admit when they are wrong. There are couples who have never confessed sin to each other, and parents who have never confessed to their own family. Why? Many feel that they will lose face before the ones who are supposed to respect them. The truth is that we only lose face when we pretend we're right and everyone else in the house knows we have blown it. The real issue is pride. And supposedly Christian parents who don't model confession of sin to their families will only raise kids who confess Christ but don't know how to walk in the life of restitution that sustains their faith.

When we boldly take a stand for God and put our actions where our mouths are, it is hard to go back. My commitment to give all to follow Christ came late one Saturday night, alone. The following days I put my repentance into practice, cutting off the ties that linked me to another way of living. Since that day I have had my ups and downs. But never has the decision to follow Christ been brought up for reevaluation. I know that this is not a result of my discipline or my determination. It comes down to His keeping power. He has treasured and kept what I have committed to Him—my heart, given in repentance. It is weak without His strength, distracted without His fellowship, and all too willing to pursue sin without His Holy Spirit insisting on my need for humility.

But each time I say yes to restitution, these tendencies are diminished, while my desire and affection for His presence and His ways increase. I know I won't finish the race without sustaining that response in my heart and actions.

10

WORKING FOR GOD

Jamie Buckingham once made a statement about working for God that resonated with me. It was something like, "Don't ever work to earn money so that you can give to the work of the ministry. God doesn't need your money. He wants you. To work for money to support the work of God is tantamount to asking Rockefeller if he needs a loan."

The issues of our work and generosity, and especially the issue of learning to work in the gift that God has given us, are favorites of mine. As a minister who receives support from others and also supports other ministries, I feel that the priority in Jamie's statement is vital to practice. I have found that when people work to support the ministry they will often take risks that are unwise, hoping that because they are investing in the work of God, He will prosper their efforts, regardless of how foolish their decisions are. Also, the one who works for money to give to God is usually not happy with his or her job.

People work for so many reasons. In our culture, it seems that most people work to stay alive long enough to retire. How boring! Why not work because we enjoy what we're doing? Of course, most have bought into the lie that this isn't realistic. But in God's economy, it is. He made us to be people whose characters are seen from our work.

Working for money, regardless of where it's going after the check is cashed, is a quick way to lose the joy of responsibility. It leads you to make decisions according to the dollar rather than godly character, such as faithfulness, honesty, excellence, and diligence. It would seem that working to support God's work would be the ticket for having joy on the job. But it usually isn't, because it bypasses a sound biblical principle—we should work to honor God with our work. If we do so we will prosper in whatever we do. And out of that prosperity we are to honor God by supporting the work of the Gospel on the earth. Did you notice the difference? Great income is the *by-product* of a job well done. Any time we replace *divine purpose* with its *reward* we are toying with disaster.

It could be argued that reward is what keeps us motivated and focused in our work. That is true. The point that could be forgotten is this—a job well done should be the *initial reward* of our work. Excellence keeps us motivated and focused, and it is also the only tract of the Gospel that some will ever read. When we complete a job that's been diluted with the distracting priority of the dollar, no matter what our intentions may be, the tract is tainted. Besides, prosperity always *follows* excellence. The minute you start pursuing the reward of prosperity for itself, you're like a dog chasing its own tail. *Don't go after the thing that was meant to follow.*

Proverbs warns us not even to consider wealth! Of all the books in the Bible to contain that warning, Proverbs would probably seem the most unlikely to the casual reader, because it promises prosperity more than any other book. Yet the warning needs to be seen in the context of Wisdom's overall view of money, which is, once again, don't work to get money—it will come to you if you give yourself to excellence. And with whatever you receive—be it honor, money, or fame—honor God.

What is the biblical command for our actual labors? *"Whatever your hand finds to do, do it with your might"* (Eccles. 9:10). This is what excellence looks like. It's not perfectionism; it's giving yourself fully to the thing God has called you to.

Another verse that speaks volumes to me is Proverbs 11:26, *"The people will curse him who withholds grain, but blessing will be on the head of him who sells it."* Notice that the man was not cursed because he didn't *give* away the product of his labors. It was because he didn't want to *sell* it! That means that our labors should contribute to the welfare of our neighbors in a sustainable way, creating profit on both sides of our business transactions.

AGING WITHOUT HEART DISEASE

Several years ago while my boys were in Senior League Baseball, I got to play in a game. It was for the kids on the team, plus their parents. It was exciting to play again. I wondered, *Do I still have it in me? Can I get out there and impress someone…anyone?* The moment of truth came. I did okay in the infield, that is, unless speed is an important factor. But at the plate…my first time up I grounded to second base. My son, Eric, was playing second. He threw me out. My next time up, I grounded to Eric again. He felt badly having to throw me out (come to think of it, he probably felt good getting the old warrior out). My last time at bat showed promise. I finally connected, and hit a deep drive into center field. It felt good.

For those who play, you know the feeling of a well-hit ball. It's difficult to explain, but you can feel when it hits the "sweet spot." And mine did. Finally, my moment of glory had come. *I can still play,* was my feeling as I approached first. Then, to my disbelief, my wife, who was playing center field, ran back, jumped into the air, and snagged the ball. My well-hit ball became her moment of glory. It seemed that *both teams* rejoiced in her achievement, knowing that it was my own family who had successfully put my once-effective bat out of business. That was the last time I played in any kind of hardball game.

I was reminded again, while playing catch with one of my sons, that I can't do what I used to do. My shoulder hurt when I threw the ball. It's not a new revelation, by any means. It's just that it's getting more and more *revealed.* I used to have a fastball. Now it ranges from slow to slower. As for running? Why should I? I'm not in any hurry.

When I was a young person I wondered how I would handle not being able to play the sports that I loved so much. Never could I imagine life without football, basketball, and especially baseball. I played my hardest. And like many others I had my share of injuries: broken bones, stitches, surgeries, a concussion, pulled tendons and ligaments, sprains, dislocated knees, casts, crutches, and many x-rays, just to keep on doing what I loved.

Getting older and losing certain abilities seemed like the worst possible nightmare. To my surprise, as much as I like those sports, I don't really miss playing them. In fact, just the thought of playing is too exhausting. I'd rather watch some-one else run and sweat. Apparently, as the body gets older, so does the heart—not the organ, but the *will* to pursue. Just think how hard life would be if the body got older and the heart got younger. We'd all be walking time bombs.

Can you imagine what it would be like if the Kingdom of God were the same as the natural world? The mature saint would be a burden instead of an asset. Our physical bodies may wear out, but that's only because they are temporal. The spirit of humanity lives forever. It grows in faith all through life. The more it's used, the more it grows. Unlike my throwing arm, it won't wear out with use. Anything that is used in the Kingdom grows and becomes more mature.

The heart is the seat of morality. It is where faith resides and grows. Our physical heart wears out. But, the heart of humanity becomes more in tune with the Spirit of God the more time we take for fellowship with Him. Some of the greatest acts of faith came when people were in the weakest physical condition of their lives. Age is God's gift—either a blessing or a curse.

There is one way to ensure that age, whether you're 9 or 90, takes its toll, causing us to sour in our walk with Christ—give place to heart disease. Heart disease is the number one killer, both in the natural and spiritual. The heart disease I refer to is mentioned in Proverbs: *"Hope deferred makes the heart sick"* (Prov. 13:12).

Disappointment is an opportunity for strength and maturity—or spiritual heart disease. It's our choice. For those who desire to be free of such spiritual sickness:

- Keep short accounts.
- Forgive quickly.
- Don't be easily offended.
- When a problem continues to haunt you and you find it difficult to let go, seek God until that bondage breaks.
- If someone disappoints you, go to the sovereign God, the One who rules the universe, and stay there until there is a healing and release.

As for me, I have since forgiven my wife for stealing my final moment of glory.

12

BUSTED!

One evening, soon after the robbery of a nearby medical building, two young men were seen running across a highway in Sacramento. As the police cars were approaching, one of them was spotted hiding in the tall grass. They were quickly apprehended and taken to the medical facility for questioning. The year was 1963. I was the one "hiding" in the grass.

It took awhile to figure out why we were being picked up. We were put into separate cars and interrogated by the officers. I remember one of them calling me a juvenile. I corrected him, telling him that I had never broken any laws. He informed me that the word simply meant that I was a young person. (I had only heard the word used with that other word—delinquent. My vocabulary grew by one that day.)

At one point an officer came into my assigned car and proceeded to tell me that my partner had confessed to the crime, and that I might as well tell him the truth. I laughed and said he couldn't have confessed to it because we didn't do it, and we were together the whole night. The same procedure continued over and over and over.

We only crossed the highway in the first place to collect a payment for my friend's paper route. His customer had asked him to come at that late hour. Why was I hiding? I wasn't. We had been running through the field next to the highway, and I tripped and fell. We repeated the story until they were convinced we were telling them the truth. When they drove us home I was happy to see that my parents weren't there yet. You see, Dad had told me not to leave the house that night. But, I thought one quick trip across the highway wouldn't hurt.

Upon my dad's arrival, I told him what happened, hoping to get some sympathy. He never had much time for self-pity, for which I am grateful. He reminded me of his rules, and that it doesn't pay to break them.

It became evident early in life that when you have praying parents, you don't get away with much. And even if you do sneak one past them, eventually it catches up to you. That is the lot in life for those who have been dedicated to God by their parents.

I sometimes laugh at Christian kids who try to get away with things. Their unsaved friends can do something for a lifetime without any apparent consequences; yet when the "prayed for" try it…"busted!"

Why does it work like that? Because the Holy Spirit is protecting what belongs to Him.

Parents who daily commit themselves and their families to God are much more likely to raise kids who make that commitment for themselves.

13

FLYING KITES

When Steve Thompson, a Weaverville church member, heard that we were going to Santa Cruz for our vacation, he thought it would be a complete waste of our time if we didn't experience the joys of kite flying. After all, the focus of my vacation is doing nothing on the beach. And the beach has wind. I always thought the wind was there to cool me off. Steve helped me learn otherwise. Wind is for flying.

Kites are different now. As a child, mine were made of cheap wood sticks covered in paper, with strips of cloth for the tail. They loved telephone wires and treetops, and had a lifespan worthy of the dime they cost me. They were fun. But that was then. I'm an adult now.

Steve traveled with me to Africa and France on a mission trip, and knew that I had an eye for anything made with quality and creativity. He had discovered a world in kites that was heretofore undiscovered by me: special fabrics, graphite poles, and strong high-tech lines. I once visited him and his family on their one-year mission's assignment at His Kids Ministry in Mexico. On the way from the San Diego airport to the orphanage, he took me by a kite store so that I could be exposed to his world. Wow! They cost from sixty to several hundred dollars. With the wind constantly blowing at the orphanage, Steve's idea caught on of harnessing and using what we can't change. Kites have become quite the rage among adults and young people alike. And now he's trying to convert me.

The sun was very hot the day of my maiden voyage. The beach was starting to get crowded. I assembled the kite with care, attached both lines, and set out to fly. To my amazement it took off with a vengeance. Gone were the days of running until you're exhausted just to get the dumb thing in the air. This kite reminded me of a horse that I once rode. It had to be put in a small corral or it would run itself to death. But I guess that's another story.

Beaches are quiet places, good for families. The Santa Cruz beaches have the additional quality of attracting an entire generation that hasn't heard the '60s are over. They are colorful individuals who, with their congas and unusual dress, make beach life a real adventure—and one that I actually enjoy. My kite stole the show. It flew with the quickness of a hummingbird and the speed of a fighter jet. This thing even made a noise that said, "I'm going very fast!" as it whizzed by. Within moments it was obvious to all that I was a rookie. Mothers ran, carrying their children to safety. People scrambled for cover. This airborne kite had the same effect on people as if I'd yelled "Fore!" on a crowded golf course. Panic. And within moments I had one whole section of the beach to myself.

Earlier in the week we watched two artists (great kite flyers) do their thing on a much more crowded beach. They carved away at their piece of the sky, quickly bringing the kite to within about a foot from the ground, only to cause it to gain maximum altitude in a moment of time once again. It was amazing. With flair they twisted and turned in the sky, much like mine. Only theirs went in circles on purpose. People watched in amazement. No one scrambled. No one was afraid. It must be nice.

I have to admit that my brief experience with this kite was fun. I had several good crashes, but no fatalities. Frightened mothers helped to ensure that my pride was the only casualty. My family recorded the event on our camcorder so that we could treasure the memory of my ineptness forever.

Learning new things can be fun. Ask any child. Yet it seems to me that many adults in the church who desire to learn, really want to get more knowledge but not have a deeper experience with God. In my book, experience is at the heart of true biblical knowledge. As long as we keep learning on a head level only, there is little chance of failure.

Could that be our problem? Fear of failure? It's only when we walk onto a beach with the possibility of looking like a fool, and scaring every reasonable person in sight with our new adventure, that we really are approaching life the way that would please God the most.

Learning new things in God is very similar to flying kites: fun, dangerous for bystanders, sometimes funny to watch, but made possible only by the wind.

14

FOOTBALL INJURIES

One day I was flipping through my most recent issue of *Macworld*. I found an article on "Safer Computing." It was filled with information on "how to stay healthy while working on your Mac" and "how to prevent injuries." I noticed after a casual glance that "tightly gripping a mouse can cause arm damage," and that there is "stress-reducing software." I realized that there are many who have carpal tunnel syndrome and other such injuries related to computing. I know the injuries are real and serious. But I'm struggling. It's difficult for me to think of pain in the workplace when that place is not at the lumber mill or somewhere outdoors. I confess, it must be a macho thing, and I'm the one at fault.

It could be a sign of my age. It used to be that injuries came from doing something. In recent years I've noticed that most of the time my injuries come when I'm not doing anything; like sleeping and waking up with a stiff neck. And then there's the injury to the back by turning the wrong way.

At one time in my life injuries were like medals of honor. We didn't look for them, but neither did we fear them. They were all part of the game. Football is that way. I had regular visits to our medical center for x-rays and other miscellaneous examinations. While the gridiron is a rugged place, I also received my medals in the sports of basketball and baseball. But football played the greatest role in teaching me about pain.

I was introduced to this great sport my sophomore year in high school. After several games, a broken hand, stitches in my arm, and continual soreness and pain, I realized that this newfound love would cost me something. It's hard to explain how you can play knowing that you may be carried off the field on a stretcher. It's even harder to explain how eager and excited one can be at the thought of giving your all for a victory. Actually, I probably could have explained it to you 25 years ago. Right now I can't remember why I used to think that way.

My junior year started with more of the same. During a practice game I was the recipient of a misdirected kickoff. I returned it so well that I earned a spot as a running back. But during the year I also had dislocated knees, a broken finger, a minor concussion, and a possibly broken nose. I say *possibly* because I didn't always go to the doctor when I was injured. I once broke a finger in baseball and felt it was unnecessary to go to the emergency room. Did I know it was broken? Yes. It looked something like an oak tree branch grafted onto the trunk of a palm tree—unique. I set it by pulling the finger straight out as far as it would go. I bought a splint at the drug store and wrapped it with white tape for that professional look. It healed up real good, somewhat like a recovering oak tree.

My coach called a time out for me during one game because I could no longer see. While lying on my back my eye sockets were filled with blood because of my possibly broken nose. As a man of compassion he called time and sent in a towel. After a brief clean up we resumed play.

Jerry Owens, the above-mentioned coach, was my inspiration. During a college game he had his front teeth knocked out. He spit them into his hand, took them to his coach on the sidelines, and went back out to finish his job. Now that's an injury. And that's dedication.

My senior year was more of the same. About six weeks were spent with crutches because of ligament damage. What memories!

The way I figure, this concept of the office being a place known for injury is evidence against evolution. It is understandable for people to experience pain in an accident that happens while doing hard work. But for us to digress to the place where we are injured while sleeping on beds that are designed by scientists and then go and sit in ergonomically correct chairs while we work, and still get hurt—this can't be considered progress.

Maybe some of us should get outdoors more often and possibly even exercise. And if the evolutionists insist that this is the evidence of our bodies adapting to our new environment, they have a poor future envisioned for us. Can you imagine what we'd be like in twenty thousand years? People would become this large brain, encased in a thin skull with few other body parts: they became unnecessary. In fact, the computer of the day would probably respond to brain waves. Talk about weird injuries. Can you imagine picking up a virus from a computer?

The concept of evolution, if not for the tragic effect on the mind of men and women, is one of the more laughable ideas of modern times. Even Darwin, late in life, considered evolution as the careless idea of his youthfulness.

Take a look around. We are not evolving. Instead this entire world system is digressing. We are going from the wonder of man walking with God in the

Garden to the eventual judgment of Satan and his followers, be they people or the fallen angels who work with him.

Only the Kingdom of God is progressing. We go from glory to glory, from faith to faith, from strength to strength, until that perfect day. Now that's progress! And the Author of such progress is the Revolutionary Evolutionist, Jesus, the Christ!

15

GAMBLING

My travels in ministry took me to the center of Nevada. Ten hours in the car is a pain to most every part of my body. Reno is on the way, and is a nice halfway point. I now break up this trip into two days' travel instead of one.

Reno is actually a great place to stay, if the local interests don't distract you. Because of the gambling, they provide great prices at their hotels for lodging and meals, hoping we'll lose our shirts in the name of recreation. The Hilton has a wonderful fitness gym, with a fair amount of weights. By staying there I can continue doing my workout routine before hitting the road.

When I called the Hilton to make reservations, I was pleased to discover they had a special deal; one night for $46, plus $15 in coins. Coins? No problem to me. Fifteen silver dollars spend as good as paper money, which means my room was really $31—a very, very good price.

When I came back through Reno I got another coupon for coins. This time I went to the appropriate place to exchange the coupons for coins and then went to the appropriate place to exchange them both for cash. The woman behind the counter asked me what I wanted, "Quarters or silver dollars?" To walk out with $30 in quarters seemed somewhat uncomfortable, so I asked for dollars. To my surprise, the coins are not real currency. They are coins minted for their machines only! I made the mistake of asking where I could exchange them for real money. Apparently, in doing so, I hit a nerve. Imagine a pit bull, eyes locked on to her next prey, angry and hungry, all in human form. You say you can't imagine it. Go to Reno. I'm sure she's still there. I was then informed that those coins were given to me so that I could gamble. I smiled, thanked her for the help, and left with $30 in fake money.

Just think, $30 to use in their slot machines. Could this be Jehovah Jireh, God, my Provider? Maybe there is a jackpot of $1,000,000 just waiting for me to take that step of faith. "Oh God, I'll split it with You fifty/fifty…I've reconsidered and am feeling real generous. You take 75 percent, and leave me with a measly ol' 25 percent (only $250,000). We could finally build our building!" And then there is also the thought that this would be a great way to "plunder

Egypt"—to take from the evil system and release it into the ministry of the Kingdom of God. And who could call it gambling, it's not even my money. Technically, it's not a gamble when I stand to lose nothing. Or, do I?

Fires, like those in California and Colorado show the potential devastation of one careless act. A house that took thousands of man-hours to build is destroyed in moments. The empires of wealthy people that took decades to create are gone in minutes. The thought of rebuilding is overwhelming at the time; many things can never be replaced.

How long does it take to build credibility and a good name? A lifetime—that is part of our life's work. And with one careless act, that work can be destroyed. Is the prospect of winning $1,000,000 worth that possible loss? Not for me. And the only thing worse than losing the previously mentioned $30 in coins would be to win the million dollars. Why? Because I would have done something that would have been published far and wide—"Pastor wins a million in Reno"—again, lowering the standard of righteousness. I owe more than that to a generation that is desperately looking for examples to follow.

Am I saying that gambling will send someone to hell? After all, it's a gamble just to drive on our freeways. No. I doubt that anyone will spend eternity in hell because of gambling. Yet greed is at the heart of the world system and is the basis for that activity. To accept that method of *earnings* goes against the whole counsel of Scripture.

What about those who gamble with a modest amount of money as a recreation? I applaud anyone who has the self-control to stop at a modest amount. There are so many who can't say no to the idea of quick wealth, and in turn put the welfare of their whole family at risk. But the real point is, it is not true recreation. It doesn't re-create anything that we want in our lives in the first place.

There is a better way. If you really want to prosper, do it the way that lasts and lasts. Take your lottery money, your one-armed bandit money, and your crap table money (somehow it seems that maybe a moment of divine inspiration came upon the one who named that game), and place it into missions, or give it to the poor. Giving is never a gamble. It *always* brings a return. In addition, it plugs us into the order and benefits that exist in the Kingdom of God. And the result is true prosperity…real *recreation*.

I was invited to return to central Nevada. When I go, I will no doubt stay at the Reno Hilton. I will eat there and work out in their gym before the five-hour drive. But, exchange my name for thirty pieces of silver? No thanks. That's been done before.

16

Hunting for Rabbits

In my growing up years, I often dreamt of living where I could hunt and fish whenever I wanted. My high school years were spent in Los Angeles, where the word "hunting" had taken on a new meaning. When my dad answered the call of God to pastor in Northern California, it didn't take me long to "bear witness" to that call.

Finally...dreamland. And "a river runs through it."

For years I had hunted only in magazines, except for a few special trips with my dad. My fishing experiences would have been most restricted to the printed page as well, except that I had a boss who loved to fish in the ocean. We went often.

The move to "Mecca," Northern California, wasn't anywhere near to what my dad and grandpa had described to me when they talked of our homeland, Minnesota. But I adjusted quickly and made new friends. Only one of them hunted. And he was more talk than hunt. It was obvious that I would have to learn on my own.

Feeling the itch to kill something (calm down, I only wrote that for dramatic flair), I left the house headed for nearby fields to hunt for rabbits. With a .22-caliber rifle in hand, I walked, looking for unsuspecting prey. And then the moment that all great hunters look forward to came to me. I spotted Mr. Rabbit seeking shade under a large bush.

I raised the gun to my shoulder...he was firmly in my sights. But something wasn't right. I lowered my rifle, just to be sure. Convinced that I had indeed spotted my prey, I raised the gun to my shoulder again. As I prepared to shoot, and increased the pressure on the trigger, something felt wrong. So I lowered my rifle and quietly approached my target. It was then I discovered that what I thought was a rabbit was instead a small child, playing. (That horrible feeling that you have in your gut from reading this can't possibly compare to the feeling that is in mine to this day.) It is amazing what you can see when you want to see it badly enough.

I was never careless with guns. We were taught to respect them (fear might be a better term). It was probably a combination of that respect and the consistent instruction, "Be SURE of your target!" that kept me one millisecond short of disaster. Whatever the reason, I am very thankful that God used it to keep that family from loss, and me from having to live with the scar caused by such presumption.

This story also has its parallels in the rest of life. What do you want? How badly do you want it? Whenever we desire something more than we desire "His Kingdom and His righteousness" we are standing at the entrance of deception. From there we can even find justification from Scripture. (It's amazing what you can see if you want it badly enough.) But when His blessings pour into our lives as the result of putting Him first, they come without sorrow and promote our relationship with Him.

"Seek first the kingdom of God, and His righteousness, and all these things shall be added to you" (Matt. 6:33).

17

SHOPPING

I'm in a mood to go shopping, but not the kind that would excite my wife. I've never understood how she can go into a zillion stores and not buy anything. All I have to do is go into one (the right one the first time, I might add), and I can compete with the government in creating debt. Perhaps when men go shopping it should be called "going buying." At any rate, I'm ready.

The psychology of shopping is an interesting cultural phenomenon. Could it be that many women go shopping as a recreational activity? I have the great outdoors, and my wife has the mall. Plus, I think some actually shop to discover what they need. My perspective is obviously all wrong. I first discover my need, and then go to the store.

Actually, I have changed a lot. As the new me, I can be in a fabric store for several minutes without making a single complaint. And my burnout time from the whole mall experience is no longer ten minutes. I can go for about an hour and a half before my wife comes up with creative suggestions as to what I should do while she goes from store to store. We work so well together that often she doesn't even have to say anything. There is a look that comes over her face that lets me know that I should find something else to do. I then get this incredible idea: "Honey, I think I'll go to the espresso shop. Come and get me when you're through." She gives me a smile that lets me know I did a good job. What a team we are!

I have several friends who shop, but their methods are much different from mine.

Mr. Research goes through all the reports on a given product. Then he talks to owners of that product to get their opinions. If it passes his scientific testing, at his price, he makes a purchase. *Pros—he buys products that last. Cons—it's too time-consuming.*

I have another friend, *Mr. Cheapskate,* who simply looks at the price tag of the desired product. If it's cheap, he will try to get it cheaper. If he can get the seller to go down in price, then he might make a purchase. *Pros—he always has money in the bank. Cons—he makes me nervous.*

And then there's *Mr. Outdoors,* who shops according to a unique set of priorities—a $1,000 deer rifle, a $3,000 hunting dog, $1,000 fishing outfit, and $200 invested in all the furnishings of his home (via garage sales). *Pros—he makes a good hunting partner. Cons—he will always be single, which most of his type call a pro.*

Mr. Blah is the ultimate bore. He says, "If they didn't need it a hundred years ago, I don't need it now!" *Pros—not likely to be robbed. Cons—doesn't own anything worth robbing!*

I like my way best. My brief research brings me to the best possible brand of product. If it fits the bill, I make the purchase. If I can't have the best (for what I need), I usually don't buy anything. *Pros—has quality possessions. Cons—is usually broke.*

Let's be honest. Who would you rather have buying your Christmas gift at the office Christmas party? *Mr. Blah?* He's likely to get you a Sears catalog. Or how about *Mr. Research?* He might have it picked out by Easter. *Mr. Outdoors* is a risk. You could end up with empty shotgun shells, and not even be a hunter. As for *Mr. Cheapskate?* He is no risk. No one is even betting on him. He is known for giving $1 McDonald's coupons. I believe I'm the only one left on the list, am I not? Why? Everyone loves quality, if someone else is buying.

Honestly, guilt sometimes gets the best of me. The spurts and changes that I've experienced with money could make one think that finances are somehow attached to hormones. A real Jekyll and Hyde. I've tried cheap because of guilt. It usually backfires, though. Like the times I've tried to stay in cheap motels to save a buck. I get little sleep. The rooms around me are often used for activities other than rest. The cheap clothes usually last as long as their price tag. Either that, or the third sleeve on the shirt makes it a bit unsightly. I've tried cheap. It's depressing.

I even became a *Mr. Research* for a short period of time. To further my commitment to the life of wisdom, I subscribed to *Consumer Reports.* But I ran out of money and time doing the research. Being wise can be exhausting.

Is there a shopping method that is morally correct? I doubt it. These methods come more from personality than morality. But materialism is a real enemy…one to watch for. Why? Our life's focus, be it Heaven or earth, determines what feeds our soul. And a soul fed by this world is never satisfied and can only reproduce corruption.

The prophet Isaiah had something to say about our focus. By the Spirit of God, he taught us how to obtain a wealth that is not of this world. He said,

"Why do you spend money...for what does not satisfy? Listen carefully to Me, and eat what is good, and let your soul delight itself in abundance" (Isa. 55:2).

Every time we quiet our hearts and listen to God, we invest in His Kingdom and feast at His table. And the only currency He will accept is a hungry heart and a listening ear. Don't leave home without them. Let's go shopping!

18

Noises

My poor wife has endured my intolerance of annoying noises for decades. I have been aware of this problem for quite a while. My kids grew up with a *nervous* dad, probably wondering why they couldn't make racket like most of their friends. As a loving parent I would try so hard to be like other dads who didn't seem to have any nerves left. It was as though they couldn't hear the cap gun going off in the house, or the squeaky wheel of the toy truck on the kitchen floor. Try as I might, I could never get a handle on the internal shakes that seem to coincidentally arrive at the same time as the noise. While I was always able to control myself and be civil, I have been somewhat dismayed by the intolerance I felt inside.

I'm worse in the car. Cars are notorious for having noises that appear only after you have signed the purchase contract. And finding them is sometimes harder than locating the criminals on the FBI's 10 Most Wanted list. My patient wife has crawled into the back seat more times than I care to admit, looking for that noise that she didn't hear until I pointed it out to her. My kids get that funny little grin that says, "Poor Dad." I think it's pity.

When I was about 9 years old, my dad and I traveled to San Francisco to watch the Giants play baseball. (He also has a dislike for annoying noises in a car. I, for one, appreciate his gift.) I was awakened that night by an incredible noise…snoring. I remember walking over to the window and looking out at the city wondering how Mom could ever sleep. And then there was the question of whether or not I'd ever get to sleep again. What a sound that was!

A woman was recently cited by her city's Noise Control Unit for snoring. Honest. It was so loud that the people in the next apartment couldn't sleep at night. The case was eventually dropped because it was ruled that it was not a noise that she could control. I understand that she is suing for damages. Apparently she was traumatized because of the experience and suffered great emotional damage.

In all fairness, I must admit that I've been known to snore a bit myself. Me, the noise hater, annoys others with snoring *a la excellence.* According to those who imitate me, my snoring has an "R" rating because of the violence.

Some people wonder how my wife became so patient and tolerant. She has this quiet quality that is the desire of many. It just occurred to me that she received that gift sometime during the *night watches*, as David would call them, probably from resisting the temptation to put a pillow over my mouth.

While she has endured wonderfully, it doesn't mean that she is not interested in finding a solution to my problem. She just bought me a special *anti-snoring pillow*. Somehow it tilts the head into a non-snoring position (which I never knew existed). It has actually worked. Even though I still don't get much air through my nose, I now don't peel the paint each time I inhale.

My mom calls me a salesman. But the thought of having to sell something makes me nervous. Yet I confess that I do encourage my friends to try the latest gizmo or tool that has brought joy, convenience, or worthwhile pleasure to my life. Be it Macintosh computers, Tiger Sauce, or now the weird little pillow under my head...trust me, you can't live without one.

At one point the disciples said that they couldn't help but speak of the things that they had seen and heard. They had found something they couldn't live without and wanted others to know firsthand. When you've tasted of eternity through a relationship with Jesus, how could anyone keep silent? And our pleasure in knowing Him grows as we give it away.

Watching a good movie is fun. Watching a good movie with friends is great fun. Going out to dinner is fun. Going out to dinner with friends is great fun. Seeing friends enjoy something is often better than enjoying it for ourselves. That must be why Jesus said, "It is better to give than to receive." He knew that the *pleasure button* inside us was pushed extra hard when it involved us actually giving ourselves away. It's the nature of life. In fact, everything that God made works properly when it gives. Whether it's talking about the sun in the sky or our families, they all give as their purpose for being.

Do you find it hard to tell others about Jesus? Just make knowing Him your priority and you'll find it hard to be silent. Religious witnesses are much like the *clanging cymbals* of Scripture (or should I say the noise in my car?). But those who know and love Him are music that the world can't live without.

Is it possible that my intolerance of noise is a godly characteristic, similar to His intolerance of clanging cymbals—religious form without love? I didn't think so...but you can't blame me for trying.

19

THE SWEATER

There was a time in my life when it seemed that everything I touched turned to gold. As a teenager I bought car parts for the hot rod that I planned on building. My knowledge of cars (including both their parts and how to work on them) wouldn't fill a page of the common diary. Yet I bought what seemed good, and sold them at very high profits...after I finally realized that *buying* was easier than *building*.

I had a paper route as a kid. Living in a new development made it easy for my business to grow fast. I actually ended up with two large routes. I hired neighborhood kids to do the things that I didn't want to do, and made good profit from their labors. Collecting the subscription money at the end of the month was boring, so I paid a friend to go with me. Such is the life of high finance.

When my family went on a vacation back East one summer, I bought many firecrackers in a state where they were still legal. After bringing them back to California, I sold them at about a 1,000 to 2,500 percent profit. Illegal? Yeah. I had little conscience for that sort of thing.

The craziest thing about all this was that money mattered very little to me. Of course I wanted a few bucks for a pack of baseball cards, or our Homecoming Banquet in my high school years. But other than that sort of thing, I gave it or spent it with equal fervor.

About ten years ago, some good friends took us to Israel and Italy. It was a trip that impacted my life in a very significant way. Many things were started in my heart on that trip that I'll not elaborate on here, except to say that a deep burden for nations began then and there.

In looking forward to this trip, Beni and I saved our birthday money so we could buy something special from one of these two countries. I chose Italy.

It was early evening in Rome. We had a few hours to shop, eat, and get back to the hotel for a brief night's sleep before hitting the road at a pace that causes my heart to race just from the memory. We were near the Spanish Steps, an often-filmed part of this great city. The shopping here was some of the best that Rome had to offer. The cobblestone streets were off limits to vehicles, except for an occasional delivery truck. Stores of notable distinction were everywhere.

When we walked by this particular men's clothing store, a beautiful sweater caught my eye. We decided to investigate. I tried it on and felt like a million bucks. After quickly calculating the exchange rate in my mind, translation their *lira* into our dollars, I came up with $110 as the approximate cost for this sweater. I don't mind saying I'd rather spend a lot for one item, come away with quality, than spend the same amount for three items of questionable quality. Still, that was more than twice the amount that I had ever spent on a sweater before. But, we thought, we're in Italy only once...go for it! So I did.

When the gentleman handed me the bill, I made a horrible discovery; that quick calculation in my mind was based on a currency exchange that I did at our hotel. I made the mistake of thinking that I had given the hotel manager a $10 bill for a certain amount of their currency—it was actually a $20. That meant that my expensive sweater was actually twice what I had previously thought. What was barely acceptable at $110 really cost $220. I was stunned. Most would probably have stopped the purchase. I was too embarrassed and proud...and stuck.

We left with what amounted to two months' income from our early days of marriage invested into one piece of clothing. The rest of the evening, while fun, was stained by an extreme case of buyer's remorse. After a taxi ride that would shame most rides at Marriott's Great America, we returned to our hotel room. I asked my wife to promise that she wouldn't tell anyone what I had just done. I kept the sweater hidden in a box for the rest of the trip. Where were the deals that seemed to find me in my youth? They certainly weren't in Rome.

Buying and selling as a hobby has long since vanished from my life. Groceries, school clothes, tuition, mortgage, and the needed repairs from my dogs' fetish with chewing, have had my attention for about as long as I can remember. I seemed to have more of those sweater experiences than in my past. I'll let you figure out why...I haven't a clue.

Today, there hangs in my closet *the sweater.* I've worn it several times over the years—probably at about $15 a whack. I had momentary encouragement when my mom saw the same sweater at an expensive clothing store in San Francisco for over $500. Today it has holes from the moths, (expensive things usually require more care and upkeep. It must be a law of some sort, but not one that I understand). While I no longer wear it, it is there to remind me of something I've learned (and have yet to learn): *"Lay up for yourselves treasures in heaven, where neither moth nor rust destroys, and where thieves do not break in or steal; for where your treasure is, there your heart will be also"* (Matt. 6:20-21).

I enjoy life. My family brings me more joy than should be legal. Whether it's taking time to write or lifting weights, helping someone grow in Christ or watching a good movie, I like it all. But there is one thing that captures more and more of my attention and affection—investing in eternity.

All who invest in Heaven have the privilege of saying, "Everything I touch turns to gold."

20

You Are So Cute!

Leah and I were driving home from church one Sunday morning. Like a typical pastor I was going over in my mind: *Who wasn't there? What could have been done better? What went well?* Leah was also deep in thought. She wanted to know if I knew the name of her dolly. She was about 4 years old at the time. I had often seen parents who were good at ignoring their children. I promised myself that I'd never be that way. But here I was, deep in thought, entering conversation sparingly. The name of a dolly?

I must admit I did not give my best to guessing the name. I never liked that game anyway. After noticing my hesitation, she asked if I wanted a hint. I gladly accepted. She told me the name started with the letter "B." With a mind full of everything but names starting with B, I sat silent. Leah is a mercy giver, especially to her daddy. She asked if I wanted another hint. I of course said yes. She then told me it started with the letter "J." My response was laughter—the kind that told her that she had done something cute, but couldn't figure out what it was. When I stopped laughing long enough to ask her the name of her dolly, she said, "Sally."

On anther occasion, at that same age, we were sitting in the living room together. For some reason, unbeknownst to me, her attention was on her brothers. She proceeded to tell me that she didn't want any boys in her room, except me, of course. I was reading. I put my book down long enough to hear her latest desire. I said something to the effect that it was fine with me. A few minutes later she brought it up again, concluding that she should now go and make a sign to put on her door: No Boys in My Room, Except Dad! Thinking it was cute, I said it was no problem.

Probably a good ten minutes had past when a frustrated little girl emerged from her bedroom. She came directly to me, with her hands on her hips, doing a perfect Shirley Temple imitation, saying, "Daddy, do you remember that I was going to make a sign for my room?" I said, "Yes, I remember." She responded, "Can I write? No!" Needless to say I laughed with that laugh that says, "You are sooooooo cute!"

Children love to learn so much that they are willing to risk looking silly. Leah knew nothing about spelling, let alone writing a sign. Yet she pretended that she did and made my life richer for her efforts. Learning, risk, and laughter seem to go well together.

Often the only difference between an average educator and a great one is that one teaches a subject, and the other teaches students. For many, our educational system has catered to kids with certain gifts and abilities, ignoring the sometimes subtle gifts of others. For example, *every child is an artist.* As they grow older, that creativity is squelched through criticism (we call it constructive) and they are then pigeonholed to express themselves where others think their gifts lie. Perhaps they just haven't discovered the best medium with which to display their art. A *teacher of children* is more likely to recognize that possibility.

One of the strongest desires in a child is to learn. It is perhaps second only to the desire to be loved. This passion is most often doused by adults who no longer have the childlike approach to learning themselves, but who insist on the child listening to what they have to say. You might ask, "What's wrong with that?" We learn more from teachers than just what they say. *Lifestyle,* with its corresponding *attitude,* is the primary message of every lesson.

Jesus, concerned about this fact, encouraged the people of His day to learn from what their religious leaders *said* and what they *did.* From my way of thinking, a rigid approach to education is how to strangle the childlike heart of learning.

Whether you're a parent, an educator, or a person who desires to communicate the love of God to this world, we would do well to learn from this principle—*the heart of every teacher must contain a child's heart for learning.* If it doesn't, we must back up and rediscover the simple nature of being a believer—becoming like a child.

I have many dreams and aspirations that are yet unfulfilled in my life. Each one takes a certain amount of risk. Other people are not the cause of my unfulfilled dreams. Pride is much more likely to be the culprit. Pride cares very much what I think I look like to you. But, when I rediscover the childlike quality of real faith, I find the heart to learn and the willingness even to look silly. (If the truth be known, we look our silliest while trying to look good to others.)

Each of my kids encourages me to youthfulness. Parenting is one of God's ways to help us stay young. It is, however, a dangerous endeavor. We either stay young or become grumps! Eric's heart of adventure, Brian's uncompromising dedication, and Leah's willingness to do right regardless of what others think, all speak to me of a child's heart, ready for learning. When I grow up, I want to be just like them.

21

FROM GUM TO PRINTERS

I walked into a drug store and noticed that the gum that I had purchased the previous day for a quarter was actually priced at 35 cents. When I mentioned the discrepancy to the cashier she called the manager. All I wanted her to do was to take my dime so that I could be cleared in my own conscience. The manager came and was awed that someone would be that honest. He mentioned that I could forget about it if I wanted to. I told him no thanks and gave him the dime, explaining that if I see to it that he gets what rightfully belongs to him, God will see to it that I get what I need. That was twenty-one years ago. And God has been faithful.

A man of God was preaching at a large crusade in a foreign country. He got onto a bus and paid his fare. When the driver gave him his change he noticed that he was given too much. When he mentioned it to the driver, the man responded saying that he did it on purpose. Why? Because the driver had been attending his meetings and wanted to see if he really lived what he preached.

Yesterday I bought a laser printer for my new computer at an office supply store. I also bought some paper and a few other miscellaneous items. I left the store; on the way to another appointment, I became curious about the total price of my bill (I have this bad habit of not looking at the bills that I sign). I pulled the receipt out of the bag and noticed that the total was $107. There was no charge for the printer. In looking through all my stuff when I got home I still found no charge for the printer. Somehow, the cashier forgot to charge me for a $1,400 printer but remembered $107 of miscellaneous items. My response? "Jehovah Jireh! God is my Provider! He works in mysterious ways!" Just kidding. There was never a moment's question of what I was to do. In fact, I looked forward to calling the store this morning so that they could correct the bill—it would provide me with opportunity to give witness for the Lord.

When I called the store, the opportunity to give witness of the goodness of God was available (an understatement!). I told the salesman that I was a follower of Jesus, and that's what He would have done. He asked me if I was Bill Johnson from Weaverville, and then stated that he wanted to meet me. He is a pastor in Burney and works at the store as his "tent making" ministry. He just happened to be listening to a teaching tape of mine on the way to work that morning. In "doing the work of the evangelist," he wisely transferred me to someone in accounting.

Who says people are hardened to the Gospel? They're seldom resistant to the real Gospel. In fact, they've been fed a distorted version of Christianity for so long that they are starving for the real thing and don't know it. Give it to them. You've got it, and they need it. And there are enough situations in life to "Give 'em Jesus" that we don't have to force-feed anyone.

From gum to printers ("little to much")...I wonder what's next? Maybe a car. I really need a car.

22

HAPPY FATHER'S DAY

I received a letter from Focus on the Family. It began with this statement by Tim Hansel: "The word 'father' is so sacred that we even dare to describe God Himself with such a term. The word 'father' is so difficult that in our lifetime we'll begin to discover only portions of its meaning. The word 'father' is so powerful that what we do with it will affect the lives of our children forever."

Fatherhood is perhaps the greatest privilege of my life. Nothing seems to match its joy or sorrow, its honor or shame. Fatherhood in itself is a call to godliness. And my greatest gift to those who call me "father" is to love God with all my heart and to love my wife as I love myself.

Beni and I taught a class for Trinity School of the Prophets entitled *How to Raise Your Children for Christ.* One of our textbooks was written by Andrew Murray, with the same title as the class (available at local Christian bookstores). I quote from it to inspire fathers:

We cannot be more to our children than we are to God.

- True faith and humility are inseparable, because faith is becoming nothing to let God be all.

- The spirit of thanksgiving is the best preparation for the altar of consecration.

- If the parent can believe, the child can be saved.

- Failure in personal godliness is the root of parental failure.

- Study above everything to make your children true—first in words and then true in heart and deed.

- Believing parent, see here the two sides of a parent's calling. Be very full of faith, and be very faithful.[1]

Fathers, read your *Outdoor Life* and *Mechanic's Illustrated,* but also read something that will affect your life for generations to come.

Happy Father's Day!

Endnote

1. Andrew Murray, *Raising Your Children for Christ* (New Kensington, PA: Whitaker House Publishing, 1997).

We Must Go

Last week I spoke in Massachusetts. (Perhaps I should say I spoke and spoke—five times on Saturday alone.) All around the world people are hungry for many of the blessings of the Lord that you and I have grown accustomed to. One of the great privileges that I have is to go and minister to these congregations. There were four churches that joined together for this past worship seminar.

Much of the New England area is still steeped in dead tradition. Yet there is a stirring taking place. And God is honoring that hunger. All of the congregations that I ministered to were fairly new. They are growing as a testimony to the hunger in that part of this nation. Their plans are for this to become an annual event.

One of my greatest desires is to train some from this body to teach the things that I teach so that more can do the "going." In fact, a prophetic word was given to me to this effect. The Lord said that I would have to train others to teach what I teach because I will not be able to go to all the places that will open up. Another note—they will not always be seemingly "significant" places. But we must go! I carry a large burden for ministry around the world, and God has given us an open door. We must go!

Along those lines, our thirteen-week class on healing was reduced to a weekend seminar for smaller churches. Some other areas we have developed ministry teams for are music ministries, marriage and family, dollars and sense, and youth and children's ministries.

THINGS OR GOD

To say that God is impressive is the biggest understatement of all time. One of the things that has impressed me the most is His concern over the little things—things that often don't matter to anyone else but us, and usually have nothing to do with eternity.

I love to fish. On a scale of 1 to 10, fishing is about a negative 5 as it relates to eternal significance. Yet, because I enjoy it, He enjoys it. Someone once gave us a fishing boat. Oh, what fun! And have we caught fish! Shortly afterward, I was able to put my tired fly rod to rest. The tip had splintered years ago, but with a temporary repair (a Band-aid) I was still able to use it. I was given a new rod for my birthday. When I went to get a new fly line ($35) the store owner gave it to me. Details that would bore you to tears, that were of great interest to me, were taken care of by Him. He is a great God.

Whether it is fishing or hunting, cooking or sewing, these can become areas where God blesses us; and through our thankfulness, we are drawn nearer to God. They may not be of great value in themselves, but seeing His delight in us is of highest importance. That single feature breathes in me vitality and a fresh love for life.

This Scripture helps to keep that issue in perspective: *"Delight yourself also in the Lord, and He shall give you the desires of your heart"* (Ps. 37:4). Where is the delight? Things or God? And again, *"Seek first the kingdom of God and His righteousness, and all these things shall be added to you"* (Matt. 6:33).

When God is my delight and the One I seek, "things" are kept in their right place.

25

DREAMING ABOUT FISH

Can you believe it? I got skunked. Several days of fishing and I caught nothing, but my kids caught fish. The teacher got taught. Of course I consoled myself with the fact that it wasn't fly-fishing, which is what I really enjoy and sort of understand. Flinging crawdads, or "crabdabs" as Leah calls 'em, has never been my idea of the ultimate fishing experience. No matter how I tried to comfort myself, the fact remains I caught zero, zippo, the big goose egg.

I took my family on my in-laws' ("in-loves," as we prefer to call them) houseboat on Shasta Lake. I did very little for a few days. It was nice. I remember sitting on the deck, in the shade, reading about catching fish. It was exciting. I could picture myself with a new rod and reel, casting with precision to those poor unsuspecting fish. In my dreams I never get skunked.

As I was reading about fishing, a fish bit my bait. Being one who is particular about the condition of his magazines, I could not just throw it down and grab my rod. I had to find a non-wet place to lay it down and then hope the fish was dumb enough to hang around after tasting metal. It wasn't.

Sometimes dreaming about catching fish is the very thing that hinders us from catching fish. We all have dreams and desires for our lives. Pursuing them is harder than dreaming them.

A poll was taken among the elderly. They were asked if there was anything that they regretted about their lives. The most common answer was that they regretted not having taken more risks. God has locked up some wonderful things within the hearts of His people. The diligent dreamer discovers and pursues them.

Prayerfully consider the following verses taken from the New American Standard Bible:

Many plans are in a man's heart, but the counsel of the Lord will stand (Proverbs 19:21).

Commit your works to the Lord and your plans will be established (Proverbs 16:3).

The plans of the diligent lead surely to advantage... (Proverbs 21:5).

The lazy man does not roast his prey, but the precious possession of a man is diligence (Proverbs 12:27).

26

Sweet Is Good

This is an alert to all health nuts, vegetarians, etc. Sweet is good! Even the Bible agrees with me. Maybe I should say I agree with the Bible. In Psalm 19, the Word of God is compared to honey—*"sweeter also than honey and the honeycomb."* Had Swiss chocolate been invented I'm sure that it would have been used by any sensible psalm writer to describe the Bible. At any rate, sweet is definitely good.

As a child I liked all vegetables—if it were corn. Today, through my wife's tutelage, I eat most vegetables. Brussels sprouts, tomatoes, and lima beans don't count. Lima beans were never intended to be a food item. They were intended to be used as writing instruments on chalkboards. Brussels sprouts were designed as rabbit toys. Tomatoes are good if they are made into catsup (Heinz only), or a non-tomato-ey-tasting sauce. Trust me, I know these things are so.

Vegetables are overrated. Fruit is the best. Can you imagine the Holy Spirit inspiring Paul to write in Galatians, "The vegetables of the Spirit are..."? Of course not. There would be no attraction to character if it were likened to a carrot. Fruit is sweet. Sweet is good.

And then there is the subject of meat. We are exhorted to eat the "meat" of the Word. Now I hate to upset the apple cart here, but He didn't mean chicken. And it wasn't fish either. He wasn't implying that the Word was like a chicken thigh or a fillet of sole. What must come to everyone's mind is a big steak! Something with substance. Don't get me wrong. I like fish and poultry. It's just that when the Bible wanted to relate the need for great hunger, carrying with it the connotation of "working for it," it referred to beef. Or at the least, venison.

I need to confess that I have one problem with a biblical inference to our diet. It says to *"desire the pure milk of the word"* (1 Pet. 2:2). I hate milk. As a child I was made to drink it. But my parents had a mercy gift—powdered chocolate. You've heard that song from *Mary Poppins*, "A spoonful of chocolate makes the milk go down." Well, that was me. It is hard to imagine the Bible being compared to milk. Yuck! That is, unless it was referring to its potential delicious state—ice cream! Why of course, that must be it. Desire the ice cream of the Word of God.

WHAT'S IMPORTANT IN THE END?

I attended Margaret Fillbeck's homegoing. The thought of having a "final day" on this earth is sobering. One of the gifts that God gave to the Fillbecks was the time between the diagnosis and death. Time to think, pray, and prepare. I call it a gift because some are taken unexpectedly. And not all were ready! But Margaret was ready!

If it were known that you had a month to live, what would you treasure most about your past? What would you think about? Would it be the possessions you've acquired? I doubt it. What about awards of achievement? Not me.

While I can't completely put myself in that position, I can imagine. Memories become very special. Friends who gave of themselves just because they loved me. My wife and children who love me, and I them. For some reason my mind doesn't go to that big fish I caught or the four-point I got in the Alps. It's people.

Do you think that there will be regrets that we didn't make better business deals? Or that we didn't buy that special home when we had the chance? It seems to me that most all of the valuable memories that we will savor in those final days will be centered on people as part of God's gift to us. It doesn't even seem natural to think of how they have wronged us. For in that moment we are the most honest as to what is important.

*For the commandments, "You shall not commit adultery," "You shall not murder," "You shall not steal," "You shall not bear false witness," "You shall not covet," and if there is any other commandment, are all summed up in this saying, namely, "You shall **love your neighbor as yourself**"* (Romans 13:9).

28

FEARFUL ANTICIPATION

As I was preparing for the day ahead of me, I again became overwhelmed with appreciation for my church family and the level of faith they have chosen to live by. Let me back up and explain.

We are in a time of crisis. That term depresses some and is offensive to others. But the fact remains that the whole nation is in crisis. And global tension is only a small part of it. I can point to many things that concern me about our nation, and our church. Yet the underlying "feeling" I have for this hour is one of fearful anticipation. I don't remember a time when I have felt more disturbed over my own spiritual condition.

My position before the church is not one of greatness. I stand simply because I've been called. But God is at work in me. And somehow, in His mercy, I see better in crisis. I pray better in crisis. The hunger of my soul grows in an hour like this unlike any other. Why do I describe it as "fearful" anticipation? Because I see God's dealings in my own life. They at times seem severe. I also fear for those who have not had ears to hear, as God has been faithful to bring exactly what we've needed, when we've needed it. Yet for many, the word has gone unheeded. And they remain with us in body only, decaying, bringing infection to the lives of those around them.

Anticipation? Yes! Finally it is coming. What we've prayed for (mostly in ignorance) for years is coming—revival. But oh the cost.

As a pastor I can always find those who are failing or doing poorly in their walks with the Lord. But always, simultaneously, there are those who are standing firm in their faith, receiving the word of the Lord, growing in grace. It is the latter group for which my heart leaps this morning; and for the other, my heart weeps. It is a tight time—financially, emotionally, and even socially. Yet in the middle of external pressure, faith in God's call upon us as a church family is to reach out to nations.

When you give and pray in time of personal need, you will not be bound to the ups and downs of this world system. Your investment is to a superior Kingdom. And from that Kingdom you will receive reward.

New Building

As I write this, a big piece of equipment is moving stumps and dirt on our property. Praise God! It is starting to take shape. As someone once said, "Believing is seeing."

What's in a building? At various seasons of my life I would have answered that question differently. Fifteen years ago I would have said, "Nothing." Ten years ago I would have said, "Little." Not having had our own facility for five years has added a little "umph" to my perspective. Today, I see it as a very useful tool. And that tool determines to a large extent the kind of services and ministries that can effectively be offered to the community, and ultimately the world. In the midst of the greatest undertaking in the life of this ministry, we are to remember that facilities are useful, but the life is in the people.

During one of our prayer meetings, Buck reminded us of the story of the building of the Temple of Solomon. God's glory was established there as a response to priests who worshiped. The result: the powers of darkness were defeated in the region because light dispels darkness. Consider the victory of the Kingdom as we join hearts and minds to face the challenge and allow the God of the impossible to build through us.

How good and how pleasant it is for brethren to dwell together in unity!
(Psalm 133:1).

30

POLTERCYCLE

A few of us were embarking on one of our famous hunting trips into the Trinity Alps. The target? Deer. We were archers on a mission.

Much planning goes into a trip like this. My pack weighed between 65 and 70 pounds. (Notice *weighed* is past tense—age forced me to learn.) When I added to that another 8 pounds because of my bow and miscellaneous items, I had a painful hike to look forward to. And then came the answer to our dreams. It was a new gizmo that was sure to help this trip become better than all the others. Charlie (my partner in crime) had access to this contraption. I had read about it in a magazine, but had never actually seen one. This gadget was a godsend. (A guy's need for the latest gizmo or gadget is often misunderstood by the females of this world who usually call it childish and materialistic.)

The drive within the man for these things comes from a desire for efficiency. We want to save time, effort, and in the long run, money...really. When a man doesn't stop and ask for directions when he is lost, it is considered to be a pride or ego problem. Wrong! It's because it is a waste of time. We know that what we are looking for is just around the corner. And when the wife asks for a food processor, why buy one that just processes? Especially when you can find one that processes, dices, smashes, mixes, juices, and will even vacuum the floor if you program it correctly. Efficiency is at the heart of the man!

For lack of a better term, this new thing that would make our hike much easier was a *cart*. Picture a short unicycle with a basket mounted on top. Then add to that two handles extending out the front and two out the back. The handles were equipped with hand brakes from a bicycle.

With such a wonderful invention our eyes were opened to new possibilities. This cart would not only help us get our *harvest* out of the Alps, it would help us get more of the necessities of life into the Alps. I thought, *It sure would be nice if we had an archery target on which to practice.* And I just happened to have a nice one; it was tightly wound straw, about the weight of a small bale of hay. We also needed the stand to hold it up, and several other important items. One of the guys who was going with us watched us load up for this trip of a lifetime with guarded enthusiasm—which means he thought we looked like fools but just smiled a lot so as not to offend. As we loaded the magical cart, we asked each other, "Why have a half-empty cart? Why not put our back packs on the cart too?" So we did. What a relief to have our shoulders and backs free from all that weight.

It wasn't very far up the road when we decided that we were very fortunate there weren't any people around—we didn't want anyone to see us. Imagine trying to push a 200-pound grocery cart, balanced on one wheel, uphill through dirt and rocks and around fallen trees for four miles. We could have saved Hollywood much money had they been there to film the expedition—no script necessary. Single-handedly we could have revived the silent film industry. Laurel and Hardy never had a finer moment than when Charlie and I fought with a cart that had a mind of its own, which is more than I can say for either of us.

We dumped that stupid cart at the halfway point. We'd probably still be trying to violate all the laws of physics by pushing the impossible uphill. I was in such despair I would have pulled into a gas station for help had there been one nearby. At the end of that fiasco I had little strength left for hiking, let alone for hunting.

As is our tradition, we got nothing—but we should have been able to at least shoot the ones that were laughing hysterically at our imitation of deer hunters. Halfway down the trail, we found the overgrown unicycle that had become momentarily possessed. (I've heard talk of a new movie being produced by horror story specialists. It's called *Poltercycle!* But then, maybe it's just a rumor.)

There is a similarity between that *overloaded cart gone awry* and the overextended credit cards in many of our pockets. The average credit card user spends about 30-40 percent more when they use plastic than when they pay cash. Why else would a business owner be willing to lose a percentage of every sale to the credit card company and have to pay an initiation fee when they agree to allow their card to be used in their place of business? It's simple. The promise of more sales.

After all, that $600 stereo for the new car isn't all that expensive when it's tacked onto a $15,000 car loan. In fact, it's just a few dollars extra a month. But unlike my magical cart, you don't notice the extra weight immediately. The pain from the extra expenditures fouls and festers until there's usually a much larger problem. I learned all this from a book—my bankbook.

Like the Scripture teaches, the key to Kingdom finances is generosity and contentment. I was ready to be generous by giving away a cart that belonged to someone else. I have since learned to be content with a half-filled backpack and a cheaper car.

31

CLEAN WATER

Picture this: I'm standing in the front row of a conservative church in Massachusetts, anxiously awaiting my opportunity to speak. This is a church I have ministered to before. Their love for God is a blessing to me. I've taken every step I can think of to prepare myself for this day. I'm prayed up and dressed up. I've put on a black suit, nothing too wild or contemporary, much like the people to whom I'm going to be ministering. I've got on my best white shirt. It is one of excellent quality with a fashionable up-to-date collar, yet it doesn't abandon the inconspicuous nature of the suit. My tie? Bright, but short of gaudy. It's hard not to allow my California roots to show. Shoes have been said to reveal the real status of a man. Mine are black slip-ons that speak of the laid-back style of California, but are of a quality that is acceptable in a dressy situation. My hair was brushed semi-carefully. Since I don't like the Ken and Barbie look (it's just not me!), I'll stay away from trying to get every hair in place.

The worship service has started. I'm ready. There is a fresh joy and an excitement for what God is saying and doing. In the midst of this setting I smelled something horrible. It caught me off guard. I've been in nations of the world where the nationals have a very distinct odor, some more *stinct* than others. I've also ministered to groups here and abroad that showered very seldom. In fact, in one part of the world it is said that Americans shower daily and shop for groceries once a week, while others shop daily and bathe weekly. I believe it. But this stench was something for which I was unprepared. I was momentarily distracted from the service as I found myself trying to identify both the nature and source of the smell. I don't know why. There was little I could do if I found the culprit.

I finally settled on *a rancid frog pond.* That was it. The repugnant smell was a rancid frog pond. As I glanced around to find the poor soul who smelled like a dead amphibian, I realized it was me. And it would do no good to keep my arms to my side. It was all over my body. If that wasn't enough to distract me, I started wondering how many others smelled it. Was it legal to pray for the well to become sick? Perhaps a stuffy nose? Not so bad that they would miss church, but just enough to block my odoriferous contribution.

It should have occurred to me much sooner than it did that I was the source of the scent. I was staying with my brother-in-law and his family. They lived on a small farm that had a problem with their water system. Their entire water supply had been contaminated by the farm pond out back. Old, stagnant, rancid water. It was green when it came out of the faucet. The smell in the bathroom that morning had been nauseating. I even debated on whether or not it was worth taking a shower. And obviously I made the wrong decision. I had hoped that Ralph Lauren's Polo cologne would mask the smell. It seemed to work for a while, but the lasting quality of Polo was not nearly as strong as Amphibian Man (something only The Addams Family would wear on purpose).

Apostle Paul taught that we are the fragrance of Christ to this world (see 2 Cor. 2:15). That is an interesting description of believers. Do we always smell that good? No. Is there any correlation between how we bathe and how we smell (spiritually speaking, of course)? I think so. Ephesians says, *"that He might sanctify and cleanse her with the washing of water by the word"* (Eph. 5:26). Words have a cleansing effect. On the other hand, words can also contaminate and infect much like the previously mentioned frog pond.

Where have you been bathing? Believe it or not, it's not hard to tell. The toxic odors of this world's idea pool have a lasting impact on its victims. If you are anything like me, you try to see if you can mask the smell of the wrong watering hole with an occasional "praise God" and a smile. Some odors are easier to hide than others, especially if you only hang around Christians who drink from the same well. Then nobody notices. That is unless you get one of those pesky, on-fire, radical, newly-saved Christians who tries to break into your group. Their whys and wherefores tend to annoy those who frequent the spiritual toxic dumpsites.

Attitudes, both good and bad, smell. It's no accident that our old nature (that way of life that exists without God's influence) is called flesh. Sweat, caused by the efforts of our flesh (old nature), stinks. On the other hand, those who are daily washed by the cleansing of God's Word and respond to that Word with obedience have a freshness about their lives. They are the *fragrance of Christ.*

I stayed and finished the series of meetings with a newfound humility. With unusual fervor, I looked forward to the next church where I was to speak. I also longed to check into my hotel and take a shower. Unfortunately, I couldn't take one long enough to make up for the days of air pollution that I caused.

I have a new appreciation for something I gave little consideration for in the past—clean water (with cologne coming in a close second). Never leave home without it!

32

Recover the Sunken Outfit

It was an unusually hot summer afternoon, and we were at the right place—Shasta Lake. Beni's parents made their houseboat available to us, an offer we gratefully received.

Imagine, there we were, in the blazing heat, surrounded by water, with nothing to do but fish, eat, swim, and sleep. It was tough.

I brought my new rod and reel that I had received from my share of our anniversary. We bought all the live crawdads we could possibly use in this lifetime, or so it seemed. Both of my boys love to fish, but Brian doesn't know when to stop. It would be over 100 degrees in the shade and he would stand there with his pole, life jacket on, sweat pouring off his face, contemplating his next move to deceive bass. And he would. Beni, a concerned mother, would *make* him go swimming.

Being sympathetic to his cause I would have all of us cast our lines into the water before going swimming. That way we could have the best of both worlds—swim, and watch our rods for any stupid fish that hadn't learned what it meant when a family of five would froth the water directly overhead. We somehow convinced the crawdads to hold on to our hooks.

During one of those swim times, I looked back and saw my rod flopping around the boat like it was having a seizure. Oh how I had overestimated my ability to get back to the boat in time to reel in a fish. I swam my fastest, only to find that it was like one of those slow motion dreams. I was moving as if I were swimming in wet cement.

My rod and reel flopped overboard, sinking out of reach.

I've learned to give thanks to God for all things…eventually. Actually, I was ticked. My brand-new outfit was gone. Someone in my family, trying to console me, suggested that I use another rod to fish for the fish that was now digesting my impaled crawdad. I was not in a mood to receive suggestions from anyone, especially someone who didn't know as much about fishing as I did. Besides, when a fish is dragging around a rod and reel via a crawdad, they tend not to eat for a while. We experts know these things.

It took a while, but I finally recognized that the suggestion was better than anything I had come up with, as silly as it seemed. I doubted that fishing for a fish already hooked made any more sense to me than it did for the disciples to cast their nets to the other side of the boat after they had fished all night and caught nothing. But they did it and caught more than they had with their own wisdom (see John 21:6).

When I stopped pouting, I picked up an inferior rod and reel, put a heavy lure on the line, and cast it hard. It was probably only my third cast when I felt this strange tug on the line. It wasn't a strong enough pull to convince me that I had a fish. But still, something was happening. I set the hook hard. Nothing. As I began to reel in the line I felt that strange little pull again. Then it hit me—my hook had caught the line of my other outfit—the rod and reel on one end and a fish on the other. As I reeled it in I had to be careful not to lose my catch.

Finally, there it was. I grabbed the newly baptized pole and tried to reel in that fish. But the moment I grabbed the retrieved rod, the fish came off. I can just see God telling that fish, "No, you can't let go yet. I know it's been fifteen minutes, but you must hold on until My son gets over his pity party and acts responsibly. And yes, I'll keep you out of his frying pan."

We fishermen are a strange lot. In our book, any fish is a good fish. I actually study how to become better. I subscribe to magazines to learn more. I watch it on TV and become inspired—all just to catch fish. I've stood in water that was cold enough to stop the flow of blood, yet it seemed warm compared to the outside air. As the water from the fishing line hit the air, it would freeze my line to the rod guides as though I had dipped the whole outfit in super glue. I've had to dig several hooks out of various body parts of my fishing partners (but not one was hooked by my cast). It's part of the joy of fishing. I've gotten wet from falling in more than once. One day I hit myself on the back of the head with a fly that could have doubled in the off-season as a 12-gauge shotgun slug. It was a new fly designed to get to the bottom of a rolling river, fast. It almost took me with it. I do all of this to catch a fish that most of the time I release.

To what length should we go to fish for men? Should we be willing to wake up early, endure cold weather, put up with physical pain if necessary, and even return to the water if we got skunked the last time out? We know the answer. The tragedy for many is, their gear is on the bottom of the lake.

There are times when our goal should not be to catch fish, but instead to recover our sunken outfit—the heart that weeps for the lost. In that case we oftentimes need to partner with another believer and use their help to recover our own heart of compassion. If you find yourself fishless because you're heartless, partner with someone who is knee-deep in the harvest.

By the way, we are not to practice catch and release in the Kingdom.

33

Braces and Socialism

After twenty-five years of procrastination, I finally did it. I took the big plunge, made the long-term commitment, and basically sold myself into slavery. I got braces. Yuck!

Parents, if you've never had them and have required your children to wear them, you've made a good choice. But the kids deserve medals.

Imagine having the Thigh Master (as advertised on TV for slimming thighs) compressed and then attached to the lips to open them so that the blades of a helicopter would not touch the cheeks, should the doctor want to take his family on a Molar Heli-tour. That's the position I was in for about as along as it takes Christmas to come for a child.

The dentist's assistant knew she had a wild one on her hands. I believe *chicken* is the old name for my type. She was as gentle as she would be if her salary was entirely derived from tips. She asked over and over if she was hurting me. How did she know about me? It makes me wonder if dentists have a hotline—"Oh, you have Johnson? He's a baby! Treat him nice or he won't return till the pain of rotting teeth brings him back."

I was worse when I was young. My parents refused to let me know when my next appointment was—I would complain and carry on for days leading up to D-Day. Therefore, I didn't find out until the day of the appointment; perhaps on the way to school (or so I thought), they would take a wrong turn, and I knew I'd been had. And that was in high school!

Now I'm an adult, making responsible decisions. And I chose pain. Weight lifting brings pain, computers bring pain, and now braces. That's because the new me is tough. Still a chicken, but tough. (A tough old bird?)

The responses of people to my mouthful of metal are interesting. One of the first to see me wanted to know why I was messing around with what God gave me. After some time I thought that maybe teeth are like cards. You get dealt a hand, and sometimes you rearrange them to your liking. I'm just a slow card player.

Soon afterward I met someone who thought I was having a midlife crisis. After all, I was 40-something. Hmm…could be. I work out with weights and watch what I eat. I don't have the sports car yet. But I hope it's soon.

Midlife crisis is not a funny subject for many. Numerous books have been written to help those who struggle with this *sickness*. It somehow comes upon men aged from 30 to about 60, mysteriously showing up, and mysteriously leaving. It usually causes a man to feel insecure about his achievements, or lack of them, and look for conquests to make him feel young again. Somehow looking for another woman is consistently at the heart of the man in such a crisis, which makes me wonder if perhaps the guy who made up the term might not have been a person needing a fancy-sounding name to excuse his lust.

I don't want another woman. I've already got the best. Maybe this disease took a detour in me and is quietly surfacing in the lustful desire for straight teeth. There must be something behind this. I just know there is.

Why do we feel better about a problem if it has a fancy name? Drunkenness, or its current tag, alcoholism or substance abuse, is called a sickness. *Is it a virus, or is it caused from bacteria?* Are there people who really believe this? Is drug abuse a sickness? If so, what then is a disease? Did you know that they have a name for people who are addicted to illicit sex? And it's not *pervert*. Thieves are kleptomaniacs. People who worry a lot and don't deal with their unbelief are eventually called manic-depressive. A young boy has total run of a school, leaving class when he wants, hitting other children when the urge strikes him, etc., because to correct him is a violation of his rights—he's hyperactive. Discipline is out of the question.

I wonder what the name is for the person who has to have a name for everyone else's problem. I'm sure it's fancy, but perhaps it should be Adam.

Can you imagine the 21st century version of the Ten Commandments?

- You shall have no other gods before Me. But of course, if you get My name mixed up and actually call me Allah or Buddha, it's okay. I'm all things to all people.

- Do not steal! That is, unless you have a chemical imbalance that influences your behavior to express your true individuality by taking what belongs to someone else.

- You shall not commit adultery…unless of course, you had an immoral parent. In that case you are not responsible. It's in your genes.

Be careful, Church. We are the only society in history that has had to have *psychobabble* from *professionals* to enable us to live the true Christian life.

The Menendez brothers brutally murdered their parents and their lawyers tried to convince the jury that it was the parents' fault. There are riots in the cities and it's society's fault. A student fails in school and it's the teacher's fault. Wake up! We have never been more prepared for socialism than now. Why? Socialism is a government for people who will not rule themselves, where security, well-being, safety, and success are the responsibility of the government.

Compare that with being a nation of individuals who are willing to take responsibility for their own lives—to insure liberty and success through personal sacrifice and labor. Remember Proverbs 28:2, *"Because of the transgression of a land, many are its princes...."* Loosely translated, *big government is the result of sin.*

Wow! Anyone who can go from braces to socialism must be in midlife crisis. I could probably be a case study. But actually, I'm encouraged by that prospect. If it's midlife, I've got half my life left to learn what the crisis is. I'm just glad it's not an end-life crisis. I don't want to finish the race wearing braces.

34

TACTFUL DELIVERANCE

Tact is defined by the Random House Dictionary as *a keen sense of what to say or do to avoid giving offense.* However you want to define it, it does not exist in the heart of a child. If they think it, it's likely to be spoken, oftentimes to the embarrassment of the child's parents.

Television's *Funniest Home Videos* showed a little girl sitting on Santa's lap. When Santa asked her what she wanted for Christmas she fanned the air away from the front of her face and said in disgust, "You have bad breath!" Similar experiences happen every day.

Some adults hold to the childlike trait of tactlessness, though I'm sure this isn't what the Lord had in mind when He commanded us to be like children. One lady came to me to borrow teaching tapes from great men of God, saying she needed them because she got nothing out of my teaching. Another brought a newspaper article and picture of some young men involved in a youth ministry for me to look at. She made special note of how clean-cut they were—suits, ties, and short hair—and they were still able to minister to youth. Those encounters were quite harmless and really much more tactful than if they had been by a child.

But my all-time favorite, however, was subtle, similar to the whistle of a bomb as it is falling—quiet at the beginning, but very abrupt in its conclusion. My family and I were attending a conference where I had been invited to lead worship. Between two of the sessions, I decided to leave my stuff in the church. When I later returned, someone had left a booklet carefully tucked away in my Bible entitled "Casting Devils Out of Yourself—A Guide to Self-Deliverance." Now that's catchy. I almost expected it to be like one of those Hallmark cards that play music when I open them, with the little computer voices singing, "Bill's got a demon, Bill's got a demon!"

As I glanced through it, I realized that most everyone I knew had demons. Under the section entitled "Some Physical Symptoms," I discovered some interesting things, such as the fact that muttering or talking to yourself can be a sign of demon possession. That means my secretary has it bad. She does both. And it must be contagious, because I have found myself doing the same thing of late.

I went on to read that bad breath can be an indication of demonic activity. That raised the percentage of possessed people dramatically, especially those outside Italian restaurants. (Does that mean that demons leave at the sight of a breath mint? If that is true, then Bram Stoker, the author of *Dracula*, had it backward. Garlic will not drive evil away. It must, in fact, invite the devil. Only a mint will bring real deliverance.)

If this kind of material weren't so tragic, it would be funny—a demon behind every bush, every problem? Actually, I wish it were that easy. Demons are fairly simple to take care of—carnality isn't. A demon is a spiritual being that influences people, situations, and environments with evil. They are real and powerful. But they are no match for the Name of Jesus!

Carnality is the influence of the old nature (our nature apart from Christ) in the Christian's life. The carnal Christian lives very much like the world, a substandard life in character and ministry—Heaven-bound, but lacking in true discernment, being worldly minded and without much reward on the Day of Judgment.

If only I could cast out a demon and get rid of all the problems of my life. Unfortunately, while carnality delights the spirits of hell, they cannot take credit for it. I get all the glory for my carnality.

Have you noticed that few people want to take responsibility for their actions? The world teaches us that we can blame our parents, society, our teachers—anyone but ourselves. When we came to Christ, we confessed our sin (meaning that we take responsibility for our actions). Then someone comes along, well-meaning I'm sure, and teaches the young Christian that we can blame the devil for it all. Or as Flip Wilson, the prophet of comedy, used to say, "The devil made me do it!"

One of the greatest bits of advice I've ever received on deliverance came from one who had been a deliverance expert. His teaching tapes on the subject have reached people all across the nation. He said if you want to find demons, look for them. You'll find them, because they love attention...even negative attention. He changed the focus of his ministry to being Christ-centered, and interestingly enough didn't run into quite as many "critters" (my personal word for them) as he had before.

If all fairness to the author of the booklet, I too have been involved in deliverance sessions where people's breath was unusually foul. I have dealt with people who talked to themselves in a very unnatural way. It would be easy to say that these could be outward signs of the devil's activity. In their extreme, they can be. But my concern is that most of those who read such a booklet just want to be better Christians. As a result, many are often grasping at the key for their personal growth. When they read that the reason they aren't more mature in Christ is because of demons, it provides a dangerously false hope while creating great insecurity.

What I have seen to date from this kind of emphasis is people who become addicted to deliverance, much like the *psychobabblist* (part Christian, part humanist) becomes addicted to the psychiatrist's couch. For most, if not all, the Christians I know, the thought of demons residing in their bodies is one of the most devastating thoughts they can have. All the confidence of being in Christ is shattered by one well-meaning but careless saint.

Can a Christian have demonic problems? Certainly. Paul warned us not to open the door for the devil's activity. But the Scripture answers the problem this way, *"Submit to God. Resist the devil and he will flee from you"* (James 4:7). Sound simple? That's the way He meant it to sound.

If you have a booklet or a word for God from someone, please don't send it signed "anonymous." You say you don't know how to be tactful? It's okay. Being tactless is not the unpardonable sin. I know this firsthand. Besides, anonymous items cause one to mutter to oneself. And we all know where that comes from.

35

PEER PRESSURE

When I was in junior high school we had a teacher who worked harder than any other. He seemed a little strange to those of us who were cool. He would go to sleep right after school, get up close to midnight, and then drive to a coffee shop and work on school stuff all night. He loved his work, which is all one needed to qualify as strange to us.

"Students, get a piece of paper, put your names at the top, and place the numbers 1 through 25 on the left column for a True/False quiz," Mr. Teacher said. I had a seat in the front row, but not by my choosing. As I numbered the paper, I decided to place the words true and false in random order following the numbers. He saw me and asked me what I was doing since he had not yet asked the questions. I let him know that I hadn't studied and that I might as well take the quiz in an unconventional way. (The reality was, it gave me a little more attention from the others who liked the entertainment value of the class clown.) Mr. Teacher became indignant that I would risk getting a bad grade just to be funny.

Now the pressure was on and I stood my ground—before he asked a single question I had answered all 25. The time came to check answers. I traded papers with my best friend, John. He was an A student, as most of my friends were. I wasn't surprised when he got 22 of 25 right. What was surprising was that I received the best grade in the class—23 of 25! Those who had worked for their grades were a bit upset to say the least. The whole class knew that I didn't know the right answers. But since our teacher had made such a deal over having to give me whatever grade I *earned*, he stuck with the agreement.

The following day we had another quiz. This time there were seven questions. The pressure was on. My friends wanted me to try it again (that force otherwise known as peer pressure). Mr. Teacher ignored me, or so it seemed, as he did not take notice of my "playing the odds" again. Al, another A student who had mastered the delicate balance of being a good student and a class clown (something I was never able to accomplish), decided to join the fun. He copied my answers, all before a single question was asked. My teacher gave the quiz. I decided at the last moment to change all seven answers, without telling Al—where I had written true I wrote false, and visa versa. We exchanged papers and went over the answers. Poor Al. He failed the test because all of his answers were wrong, which also meant that I had answered all seven questions correctly! He was smart, and could have done well on the quiz. But he decided to be funny instead. His mother should have warned him about peer pressure.

That was the last time I tried that trick. I actually became a fair student, though I talk about it very seldom. My blunders are much more entertaining.

The psychology of peer pressure is quite fascinating. It is generally brought up in light of what teenagers face. Yet peer pressure is not reserved only for the young. Adults face it every bit as much as do our youth, though it may show up differently.

I watch it at the gym. There are cool people, and then there are the not-so-cool (NSC) people. When the cool people express an opinion, which is usually a strong one, they are much more likely to have others agree with them than the NSCs. If two people share the same joke, one cool and the other NSC, the coolest person gets the bigger laugh.

Peer pressure exists in the Church as well. If someone is teaching a Bible study and there is someone in attendance the person really respects, the teacher will often talk to that person as though he or she is the only one in the room. Anytime a point is made, the teacher looks for agreement or approval from the respected person.

It would be hard for some to admit that many of our likes and dislikes have been shaped by people we admire. For many, their favorite color is the same as their most admired friend. For others, they have the same toys (boats, motorcycles, etc.) as their friend. I find this interesting, as I've seen it in me too. It seems that it is born from a desire for identity and approval.

Can this pressure be positive? I think so. It is what makes accountability work. If you know that you have to answer to someone for the way you eat, how you spend your money, or whether or not you've read your Bible, etc., you are more likely to make a good choice. It's human nature.

Proverbs has a lot to say about carefully choosing the kind of people with whom we spend time. The pressure to conform was never condemned. The kind of friends we choose is addressed. The scare reality is that we become like the people we spend the most time with, whether good or bad.

I only wish that I could get Christians to be more aware of God throughout the day. What kind of decisions would we make if our awareness of God became our peer pressure?

Looking back on my youth, not all my decisions were actually because someone else was doing it. In fact, many decisions were because they weren't. But then, I guess that too can still be called peer pressure. Though I got the laughs, they got the last laugh, because they got the education.

36

LONG LIFE

I don't remember his name, but he looked like Father Time. He had long, shoulder-length hair and an equally long beard, which were gray with a slight yellow tint.

Soon after moving to Weaverville, California, we were greeted by this interesting gentleman. He informed us that the previous pastor and family allowed him to stay in their home whenever he came to town. Not wanting to mess with tradition, we invited him to stay with us in the same way.

He was a piano tuner. His visits to our community were as often as he could arrange enough pianos to tune to make the drive worthwhile. I'm not even sure where he drove from, although I probably knew then. The writer of Hebrews tells us to be sure to be hospitable to strangers because you never know when you might entertain an angel. He wasn't one of those.

On his last visit I noticed his car parked in front of my house as I drove into the driveway. After parking my car, I walked toward him. I noticed his body slumped toward the steering wheel. Fearing the worst, I approached the driver's window. Sure enough, he looked very dead. In the long seconds that followed, I tried to figure out what to do.

Find a pulse came to mind. As I began to reach for the car door, his head sprang up as though his puppeteer wanted to see what I might have had for lunch. I'm sure I looked like death warmed over to him. In the brief moment that it took for him to realize who I was, he reached for a small container next to him on the car seat. And then, as though he were doing a television commercial, he raised a bottle of vitamins and proceeded to tell me that those little pills were the secret to his alertness and high energy level.

That whole scene, from my car to the sales pitch, took maybe two minutes at most. It would have been more fitting on "Saturday Night Live" than in the church parking lot in front of my house. It took all the self-control I could muster to keep from laughing myself silly. A man who looks older than dirt and appears ready to be buried in it, suddenly jumps to attention attributing his high energy to a bottle of pills. What energy?

Every once in a while I hear a news report of someone reaching the 90- to 105-year mark and sharing his or her insights on *how to have a long life* for the rest of us. One gentleman swore that eating a whole onion (raw) every day was what kept him alive so long. Another spoke of his daily cigar as being the key. And to my delight there have been more than a fair share of those who attribute their longevity to obeying God. There have also been those who have claimed that no alcohol in their lives made the difference for them. And about the time I'm ready to shout amen, someone who is 100 years old will testify that his glass of whiskey a day has kept him going strong. For others it's their vitamins, a vegetarian diet, and so on.

I'm reminded of the husband and wife team who took a tour of Heaven upon their arrival. After several minutes of being awestruck over the majesty of it all, the husband broke his silence with, "You mean we could have been here five years ago if you wouldn't have fed me those oat bran muffins?" I guess it's all relative.

Years ago I received a letter from my Grandma Johnson. She wrote, "I'll be 95 in October." When you get that old you tend to count the birthdays like a marathon runner counts the miles; every tenth of a mile counts toward the finish line. She is a spunky woman of God. When she prays, everyone within shouting distance knows she's praying. Her boldness kept her firm during a time when being a Pentecostal brought scorn and persecution. It mattered not to her. She had tasted of another world, and no one could take that from her.

She wrote, "...the Lord has been very gracious to me to give a long life and the end is not yet. I am enjoying good health. However, one day the Lord will call me up higher, but right now I am enjoying all of my over 94 years and I'll be satisfied to stay on Planet Earth as long as He wants me here. But when He says, 'Come up higher,' believe me, I want to go. But until then my heart will go on singing His praises, thanking Him for every good thing He has given....

"There's nothing else to look forward to but what God has in store for us up ahead, generation after generation. Praise the Lord.

"I somehow can't put it into words as I feel, but suffice to say, we'll go on loving and serving the Lord and believing Him to move in generations ahead—and I know He will."

In her four-page letter, she spent about three pages talking of Heaven and the goodness of the Lord. The other page was used to send greetings, thanking us for a picture we had sent, and also reminding us of God's blessing on our family. Long life without quality of life is of little value. By quality, I'm not referring to good health, although that has obvious importance. *Quality* refers to the condition of the heart. Her thankfulness keeps her young. The absence of criticism and anger has not only probably added years to her life, it has added a quality of life that even the rest of us can draw from. Just as there is no bitterness in Heaven, so there is no bitterness in the heart that is feasting on Heaven.

I take vitamins, eat the oat bran, lift weights, and do other things that are associated with good health. But above all, I think I'll follow Grandma's lead and be thankful, leaving no room for bitterness to take root.

SMALL THINGS

My favorite movie plot is with good guys and bad guys, heroes and villains. I'm not particularly thrilled over the "Batman" type film, but I do like a good ending with justice being served.

It is said that everybody loves a hero. We love to see someone take center stage in a crisis, bear up under pressure, and deliver the goods. Sports figures, politicians, religious leaders, movie stars, police officers and others often get the spotlight in our search for heroes. But what is a hero really made of? We have witnessed the reputation of great athletes turn to dust as their gambling or drug habits are revealed. Politicians and religious leaders have embarrassed both themselves and their colleagues through the exposure of immoral practices.

While the public cries for liberty among "consenting adults," the law of the heart still has influence on the choice we make of who is to be our hero. Momentary greatness is exalted, but history remembers consistency. Achievement is applauded, but character is written in stone. Heroes of lasting quality become such because of what they do in the dark. It's the small things that count. Abraham Lincoln is remembered for returning a borrowed book as much as his political decisions. George Washington told the truth about his encounter with a cherry tree and it is hallowed in our history textbooks. Consistency in small things counts.

We could live without athletic achievement and another summit meeting. But the things that make up the life of a hero are essential for daily existence, like talking kindly, loving our family members, paying taxes without complaint, serving when no one is looking or begging, being generous, thinking positively, depending on God—all are part of an endless list that comprises true greatness.

Remember, take charge of your life by thinking small. It's the small things that count.

38

MAGAMANIA

Six days of the week are like Christmas for me. That's how often I usually go to the post office. When you receive as many magazines as I do, there's a good chance that today will be the day, again. My family sometimes wonders about my collection, as do a number of my friends. I've been called a pack rat. And I've been called worse.

Actually, I've had to cut back on subscriptions. I don't ride my mountain bike enough to justify subscriptions to three such magazines anymore. Now I just buy one off the rack when I'm inspired.

I love chocolate. Finding *Chocolatier* magazine several years ago was an amazing discovery. But I haven't been reading it enough to convince my budget-conscience heart that it was more important than say, *Muscle Media 2000.* And while lifting weights has an influence on a good part of my life of late, it hasn't replaced chocolate. At any rate, I didn't renew *Chocolatier* for this year. (But I do have many back issues to read, including their premier issue.)

On top of all the magazines I receive in the mail, my secretary supplies me with many from her house. It seems that her husband has the same problem I do. I'm sure that a doctor somewhere has a good name for it: probably magamania. Or is it magaitus? At any rate, I have not found a cure, and I've not looked for one.

It seems that with every new interest, the latest being Macintosh computers, there is a monthly magazine that satisfies my hunger for the knowledge that informs and inspires. With the advent of desktop publishing, periodicals of the most unique interest became available. So whether it's dogs trained for hunting, or the latest in fake fingernails, there's a publication somewhere to satisfy your interests.

Speaking of Macs, back when there were only three different monthly publications (that I knew of) that dealt exclusively with the Mac, guess how many I received? Only three. After all, if I subscribed to two, I might miss something.

Fly fishing magazines fill the largest part of the storage built into my closet just for those paper treasures. I have been saving them for twenty years. Just think what fun someone will have when I die. They'll probably be muttering to themselves something like, "People wouldn't have thought him to be such a man of God if they saw this closet. After all, cleanliness is next to godliness, and this place is a mess." I guess maybe I should put something in my will about who gets to go through my closet. If a fly fisher of distinguished taste were to go through my collection, he would no longer have difficulty with joy.

My collection is unique. I have several premier issues. In this assortment are several newspapers of note, including *San Francisco Examiner* post-Super Bowl editions—definitely a collector's prize.

What is it about a magazine that I find appealing? Two things: One, pictures. I learn from pictures much quicker than from words. Two, because they are published at least once every two months, they provide current information—well, they did until the advent of the Internet. Technology is in constant transition. Only the Bible is static. Everything else changes.

The Bible is very much like a magazine to me. It is always up to date—more so than our daily newspaper. And with the Holy Spirit, pictures brought to mind are fabulous learning tools. And besides that, where else can you go get *life* from reading?

How do you read the Bible? There are so many different kinds of Bible readers. There's the *I'm going to get a new revelation* Bible student. He feels that because he has all the study tools that money can buy, there is nothing hidden that won't be discovered. He hasn't learned that the Bible is a closed Book—revealed, not discovered.

Then there is the *social scientist* who believes that a dose of the Holy Writ now and then will keep him with some good old fashioned values. To him the concepts contained in the Scriptures are just more good thoughts and social creeds. It never touches his heart—where the root of sin lies.

We can't forget the *dime a dip* reader, who dips randomly into the Book for a dime's worth of God. And for a moment, the religious conscience is eased. By the way, how much is a dime's worth of God?

What about you? James describes the way it ought to be: "*...in humility receive the word implanted, which is able to save your souls*" (James 1:21 NASB). Humility means dependency. It means hunger, which recognizes need. What does God expect from us? "*To do justly, to love mercy, and to walk humbly with your God...*" (Mic. 6:8).

To read anything in print today (except the Bible), you have to know how to eat the meat and throw out the bones. There is a lot of junk in print and on the

Internet. My approach to this is simple. I want to learn all I can, no matter who it's from. Why? If something is worth doing, it's worth doing well. And if it's worth doing well, it must be done for God. When I read a "secular" magazine, on any given subject, I feel as though I'm plundering Egypt.

Humble yourself. Be willing to learn from anyone, even those who don't know Christ. Use the opportunity to grow in your ability to relate to those without salvation. But by all means, plunder Egypt by taking what they know and using it for the King and His Kingdom.

39

THE BIBLE IS PRACTICAL

Yes, I am the not-so-great White Hunter. I started early, like many other young boys, reading *Outdoor Life*. At the age of 11 I had my own subscription. This magazine had a tremendous impact on my daydreams.

I even remember the day I passed my hunter safety course: December 15. This continued to be a significant date as it also became the day that Beni and I were engaged to be married. It was also my grandfather's birthday—a truly significant day. What memories!

My hunting expeditions consisted of frequent trips to "the fields"—a couple hundred acres that would someday become a subdivision. But until then, it was my Africa.

I carried a pump BB gun, the weapon of choice, proudly into the field. It had a genuine wood stock and became the envy of all my friends. We would practice and practice. Occasionally we even hunted with a bow. And quite honestly, it mattered very little what we used—we hunted both with equal success. (Fun would be a better word.) We dreamt of getting that jackrabbit, or if we got real lucky, the rare pheasant. Unfortunately we never got lucky (unless you're the rabbit or the pheasant *a la rare).* As I learned early on, hunting rarely involves shooting.

Preparation is a big part of the hunting experience. As an adult my preparations cost more than as a child—proper clothing, equipment, and reading material. It reminds me of the saying, "The only difference between men and boys is the price of their toys." Come to think of it, I never did like that statement.

Because I didn't enjoy reading books, magazines helped me prepare for the great outdoors, but not completely. I soon discovered that while reading is good, it can't possibly prepare a person for everything he or she might encounter.

A friend and I went on a 10-year-old's version of a safari. Never knowing what kind of game might be lurking in the shadows, we walked alert and attentive to any movement or noise. As we approached the brush that grew near the frog-infested creek, we heard movement in the weeds. We became silent as I readied myself for a harvest—I was the one with the weapon.

From only a few feet away emerged this wild beast—a skunk. What happened in the following moments was something that would have seemed funny had it been on *Spanky and Our Gang*, or perhaps the *Three Stooges*. We were *sprayed*. And unless you have had the experience, don't even think you know what I'm talking about. The smell was only part of the ordeal. We could taste it. It stung our eyes. And unfortunately, it became us. We ran home for deliverance.

My dad greeted me with laughter, and I was not allowed into the house for a while. I had to bury my clothes in the yard. I already had a flattop haircut, so there was little to cut that might have absorbed the odor. Had someone only written an article in *Outdoor Life* that would have warned me of the impeding danger, I might not have had to go through that horrible experience.

There is a term used in the Body of Christ—*practical teaching*. Most are weary of hearing things that do us little good. When practical means *insightful and applicable*, it is a good thing. But it has become the handle that is used to justify our preference of one teacher over another, saying, "He's so profound and practical." If someone gives a lot of formulas in their teaching, all the better. We do love following steps 1 through 4 to get our desired results. It gives us a sense of control. I personally believe that is our inclination toward the law over grace. The desire for law is seen in our hunger for preset boundaries: *"Then they said to Moses, 'You speak with us, and we will hear; but let not God speak with us, lest we die'"* (Exod. 20:19). Grace on the other hand is at the heart of a personal relationship with God where we are willing to learn as we go, never fully understanding where it is we are going.

According to the cry of much of the American church, the Bible is not very practical. There are so many important things that it never discusses. Why, for example, are there no formulas for learning how to forgive, or how to deal effectively with our past? Why aren't there more teachings in Scripture that deal with cults? The list could go on and on. It just deals with them with statements like, *forgive from the heart* and *by their fruit you will know them*, etc. While that may not be to everyone's liking, it is the truth, and it works. It's amazing how many of life's troubling circumstances can be addressed with the statement, "Trust God." Or how many things are included in the verse, *"In everything give thanks"* (1 Thess. 5:18)? What seems to be impractical is in fact extremely practical.

The Bible seldom teaches methods. But it always addresses the heart. That being the case, many consider teachings that address the heart without giving a method as impractical teaching. Is it? Or is it more impractical to give a formula that will not endure the test of time, bringing more disillusionment than strength and faith?

The Bible is practical in the right way. The rich and poor, intellectual and mentally handicapped, powerful and weak, all can live the Gospel with equal success. Don't fret when the *New York Times* or *Time* magazine reports that Judas Iscariot was a fictional character or that the resurrection never happened. Long after these periodicals are gone, the Bible will live as a testimony of God's faithfulness to humankind. Emperors and kings with great armies have marched against it, hoping to destroy its power. Philosophers have declared its end. Satan himself has tried in vain to destroy the effect of His Word, but to no avail. It will stand forever, which happens to be practical enough for me.

So I guess our motto ought to be K.I.S.S.: Keep It Simple, Saint.

And by the way, if in your walk with God you get sprayed by a skunk, don't blame your teachers. Take it as your God-given excuse to buy some new clothes.

PRAYING LIKE CHILDREN

Salmon have a drive to spawn in the river they were born in, geese fly south for the winter, and humankind talks to the Creator. Praying is so instinctive that one has to learn how *not* to pray. A child does it naturally. It's only when one is taught that there is no God, or perhaps He exists but He's not concerned about us, that people reject prayer. As Mario Murillo pointed out to us years ago on The 700 Club, the one thing that makes common television shows unrealistic is that people don't pray when crises come. Same in the many recent so-called "reality shows."

In the Body of Christ, we have dissected and inspected prayer as a subject. We've analyzed it, studied it, and talked about it. Unfortunately, the more we work on this topic, the more we tend to make it complicated. I am one who teaches on prayer. And I must ask, have I made the simple difficult? If so, how?

Some of the greatest books on the subject were written by the men and women of God from a previous generation. They were devoted in a way that is almost unheard of today. Their intensity is noteworthy. But for some of us, it is also overwhelming. That certainly is not the fault of those saints of God. It's just a response of a few of us who are scared by the apparent demands for perfection.

Prayer has at least two elements. One is *romance* or *the adventure of knowing God,* and the other is *discipline*. Understanding the two and how they are to fit into our lives can help us become mature in prayer. Failing to understand this is almost a guarantee of repeated failure.

I love my wife. There are certain traits that help make a good marriage that come naturally to us. Very little thought is needed. There are other areas that don't come quite so easy, and yet are important for us to have the kind of success in marriage that we desire. That's where discipline comes in. Without work and discipline we couldn't develop maturity in our relationship. Yet any marriage that has discipline without romance is sterile. Prayer is to be an adventure first. Then through discipline it will grow to maturity.

For the larger part of my life I have felt that the meat and potatoes of prayer was the hour alone with God. And who would dare argue against spending time with God? Certainly anyone with an understanding of the subject would applaud such priorities. For me, the icing on the cake was the fact that I could fellowship with God throughout the day.

My thinking has changed over the years. While the hour with God has immeasurable value, fellowship with God (praying without ceasing) has grown in my personal priorities. Where it once was the icing, it has become the meat and potatoes. What does that mean? For me, the constant fellowship with God is the romance. It is what makes me look for the hour to be alone with Him. When it's the other way around, the hour becomes more of a chore—that which I'm supposed to do to be a good Christian.

Children, with their innocent approach to prayer, should become the standard for us. They think nothing of praying at any time, all the time, about the silliest of issues. I think God likes that. It's not religious, like we adults tend to be. Many learned in school to give the answer that the teacher wanted us to give. We felt that to be smart we had to think and act like others, often sacrificing honesty. Likewise, many pray the things that they feel they are supposed to pray, hoping to appear right in God's eyes. As a result, few people know how to be honest with God. Not so with children.

So how do we return to the heart of a child?

- First, it takes honesty to recognize the need. Not just the need of prayer—we are conditioned to acknowledge our need of more prayer. We must recognize our need to become like children— simple and honest.

- Second, we must humble ourselves and take on the heart of a child. How? A child sees. Their eyes are open to the world around them in a way that adults often cannot see. Pressures often direct our thoughts toward bills, deadlines, conflicts, getting more organized, fixing what's broken, and preparing to fix what's not broken, ad infinitum. The burden of life blinds us to the opportunities of life. Children appreciate more simple things, like the shape of a cloud, or the box that their new toy came in. Their eyes drink in everything around them. If you move a picture on the wall I may not notice, but a child will. Life is an adventure for them, and is to be for us—with Jesus Christ at the center. Open your eyes—there's adventure all around you!

- Third, simplify. Life is only complicated when we alter what He made. It wasn't complex when He gave it to us. For example, take the subject of the law. God gave us Ten Commandments. For a people determined to serve Him, it is sufficient. But in this society it takes many volumes to interpret one simple law. How uncomplicated is it supposed to be?

Love God...and your neighbor as yourself. Give Him the *first* and the *best*, and seek to bless people with the rest.

41

My Job

This morning I had the joy of filling out the warranty card for my new Apple computer. The questionnaire was fascinating to me. They wanted to know, "What is the primary business of your company/institution?" Following that was a list of things to choose from. There was Business and Legal services, Agriculture/Mining/Construction, Manufacturing and many others. The one that stood out to me the most was Higher Education. As a pastor, that seemed the most appropriate. After all, I teach—and how much higher can one go than God and His Word?

The next question I found equally intriguing: "Which one of the following best describes your occupation?" Jobs like General Office/Administration, Sales, and the Military were mentioned. The one that seemed the most logical to me was Special Education/Rehabilitation. Teaching God's Word is most special, and it does renew and refurbish us—spirit, soul, and body. Oh, what a job!

Sometimes I feel guilty for calling "pastoring" a job. It's so much more than that. It's such a privilege to be one. So much so that no one in his right mind would choose it as a career. Believe me when I say, I never chose this job (line of employment, occupation, gifting, place of service, etc.). I was drafted—joyfully. It is also too "holy" to call this just a job. Of course there are many who would agree with me for entirely different reasons. After all, who wouldn't want a job where you work only one day a week and golf the rest? Those, however, are just rumors. There are days where I would be satisfied if I could just remember where the golf course was.

Yesterday was one such day. In the midst of some trying situations, my computer arrived. I opened the box with the anticipation of an 8-year-old getting his first BB gun. I plugged it in and began to work on deciphering computer babble, following their tutorial carefully. (One needs a very special gift of interpretation to understand computer babble. But your anointing doesn't have to be as strong with a Macintosh. That's why I bought one. I am weak in the gift of interpretation.)

I have wonderful Bible software to install, but can only learn so fast. The chapter on "Installing Software" was many pages ahead of me in my manual, so

I called for help. Without a friend's assistance, I would probably be staring at a wall somewhere, mumbling something about how the megabytes encouraged me to believe that one day I would know what I'm doing.

After the day was over, probably unable to find the golf course, I knelt to pray and then went to bed. With the strange mix of events from the day still etched in my mind, I gave more thought to what God expected of me. After taking a bit more time to pray, I came to a familiar conclusion and confessed it to Beni, "We just have to trust God." She agreed.

No matter the job, trusting God makes it a privilege with honor. No matter the problem, trusting God brings the supernatural to an otherwise too natural situation. And whether it's computers, pastoring, or an impossible-looking situation in your life, trusting God is where joy begins.

42

THE EXPLODING BRIEFCASE

Well, it happened again. Major embarrassment! It seems to be the season for feeling dumb.

We sold our Toyota, and it required a quick trip to Redding to sign the necessary papers. I then drove to the lending institution with the certified check to pay off the loan. Several hours had passed before I realized that I had forgotten my briefcase at the bank. Beni kindly went to Redding to retrieve what I had absentmindedly left, only to find out that the bank had waited for quite a while for someone to call and claim it. But because no one did, they got suspicious and called the bomb squad. The police came and carefully took my briefcase out to their canister and blew it up. My briefcase! Filled with my Bible, some study notes, and a few bills.

I was glad that the newspaper didn't get hold of the story as potential headlines flashed before me: "Absentminded Pastor Causes Terrorism Chaos." Or how about, "Briefcase Blown Up as Terrorist Precaution—Pastor Blamed." As if it's not bad enough to face the embarrassment, the bank insisted on buying a new briefcase for me. Rather I should have to pay for their stress counseling for at least a new bottle of Excedrin.

Why do things like this happen? Who can I blame? Do you ever ask yourself after something embarrassing, "God, why didn't You prevent this?" Perhaps you don't, but I do. I can just hear the Lord say, "Don't blame Me. I gave you a brain." I'm still human, and as such I still get the joy of experiencing life as it comes along. I forgot my briefcase. Try as I can, that's all the spiritual lessons I can squeeze out of it.

All of this has added new meaning to the phrase, "I'd forget my head if it wasn't screwed on tight."

43

Where You Look

One day while in Redding I thought it would be nice to look at a new car. We couldn't afford one, nor was it a proper time for us to shop. But I reasoned that it wouldn't hurt to look. We drove into a dealership that sold the particular car I had come to appreciate. The salesman graciously offered us the opportunity to take it for a test drive. We accepted. I got behind the wheel, and took notice of the amenities—velour interior, stereo, and all the other extra features that we needed so much. As I began to pull out of the parking spot, our 3-year-old son, Brian, began to sing, "Be careful little eyes what you see..." Needless to say, that was a joyless test drive. The prophet had just spoken, and I was pursuing something forbidden.

I heard of an artist years ago who would not look at a bad painting twice. When he saw a poor piece of art, he would turn his head, never to look at it again. I do the same thing. I record every 49er football game. If they lose, I refuse to look at the game again. However, if they win, I watch it at least twice, and sometimes more.

This time of year is perhaps the season with the most potential for blessing. It is also the season for the greatest temptation. David, the man after God's heart, wrote several things about where we look. In Psalm 101:3 he writes, *"I will set nothing wicked before my eyes,"* and in Psalm 123:1, *"Unto You I lift up my eyes."* This adds a new dimension to the phrase, "Keep looking up!"

P.S. No, a 49er game is not wicked.

44

PTF

There is a new PTF in town. No, it's not in competition with the Christian school's Parent Teacher Fellowship. While it is a "fellowship," it's not based upon our children. Our PTF stands for Prime Time Fellowship. It's for those who are in their prime.

For a gymnast, prime is usually between the ages of 12-19, depending on whether you are male or female. In football, prime is usually from 25-30 (except for Joe Montana—yeah 49ers!). In the business world, the prime age seems to be in the 40-55 range. And for bearing children, it's between 20-30 years of age. Prime means different things to different people. But for our church, "prime" is associated with age, and with age comes wisdom, experience, and maturity.

One of our sons visited the home of another young boy in our community. One of his first comments after returning home was how meanly they treated their grandmother. The world is losing its perspective on the value of years. In the Kingdom of God, years are to bring respect and honor. And so our Prime Time Fellowship is for the part of our church body that is more mature. (That's the diplomatic way of saying "old.") Seriously, whether you're 55 or 105, you're the part of the body that has the most to offer.

I foresee a great army of older believers being tapped for ministry in ways we never thought possible, from the very growing responsibilities at local churches to the increasing opportunities in other countries. This is my prayer.

Gather the people together, men and women and little ones, and the stranger who is within your gates, that they may hear and that they may learn to fear the Lord your God and carefully observe all the words of this law (Deuteronomy 31:12).

45

IN A SMALL TOWN

For two days, The 700 Club interviewed Mario Murillo about the Jesus Movement of the '60s and '70s and the revival that seemed to be imminent for the United States in the '90s. Whenever I hear a man of God speak words of faith with foresight, I am blessed beyond words. And this was such a moment for me.

As I look over the past few years, I am touched by the fact that God has been so good to us to bring us the best. The men and women who travel the globe, speaking in leadership conferences, ministering to children, and those who feel a burden to reach the masses—I am thankful for each one. What has made them great men and women of God is that very quality that takes them to the far reaches of the world—the vision to see what God sees, and not to be impressed by numbers. Each one has a heart to honor and build up the believers of His Body. I am so grateful—grateful for the encouragement of those who are further along in this walk of faith than me. And I take it to heart.

During this Christmas season I am reminded of Christ's humble birth. In a small town, insignificant to most, the King of kings and Lord of lords took on flesh and blood as a baby. The greatest story ever told began in a small town. The greatest man, the greatest power, the greatest movement of all was born in the smallest of towns—not fitting in the eyes of men and women.

But God's ways are not our ways, and His thoughts are not our thoughts. And so we share the miracle of destiny—the destiny and purpose that only God can give, which is to be world changers.

As we celebrate this greatest of seasons, let's prepare ourselves for a new "decade of power." This new thing that is coming upon the Church will begin with a body of people who will forsake all for the Christ we have come to worship.

Brokenness is our greatest strength.

Humility is our greatest honor.

And inability is our greatest opportunity for power.

46

THE WHOLE STORY

I had the joy of reading an unbiased periodical called *The San Francisco Sporting Green.* Within just a few pages I was able to find and delight myself in six articles on the 49ers. I don't understand why other periodicals like the *Los Angeles Times* can't write with such objectivity. While I must admit the temptation exists to continue on the Niners, something else caught my eye.

On page two of the sports section there was a "Marlboro Sports Highlight" that used the act of pitching a baseball as a vehicle for advertising cigarettes. If that wasn't already an odd enough combination, under it was the following: "Surgeon General's Warning: Smoking By Pregnant Women May Result In Fetal Injury, Premature Birth, and Low Birth Weight."

Now I realize that there are some women who read the sports page. And I wouldn't even want to imply that to do so is not proper. But facts are facts—few women read it. Especially cigarette ads that teach "How to throw a fast ball." Why would a tobacco company want to place that particular warning in a place that is seen predominantly by men? Why not print, "Warning: This Stuff Will Kill You!" Marlboro was able to successfully dodge the issue of giving bad news to the people it involved.

I'm glad that Jesus didn't skirt life and death issues. He spoke freely of eternal hell and Heaven. He didn't say to the Pharisees, "I know your intentions are good; thanks for the help." With compassion He reached out to all who would be touched by His life. But for the rest, in mercy He warned of a coming day of eternal judgment.

Even to His followers He spoke about us having to answer for our choices and words. As His disciples, we have "good news and bad news" to share. Let's give people the whole story. It will help some to see the good news in a new light.

47

LOVE CASTS OUT FEAR

What would you think if I told you that I have personally encountered a terrorist group working in Weaverville? What would your response be if I were also to add that on occasion they were able to infiltrate Calvary Chapel and use its members to carry out their evil schemes?

Living in a small town removes from most the natural suspicion that such a thing could happen. Yet that is a false sense of security, because the above is true. Least I be accused of over-dramatization, let me clarify three things. One, they are extremely powerful and have networks all over the country. Two, they are determined to overthrow the government that rules over us. And three, because it is spiritual in nature, it is a greater reality than that of a man with a bomb.

The name of this terrorist group—Fear.

It's not a group of reckless people, but a movement of demonic beings trying to bring about a collapse of the Kingdom of God. Not by a military overthrow, but through a subtle influence in the minds of those whose lives depend on the love of God and the faith that conquers the impossibilities they face. That movement is failing! Hallelujah!

Jack Hayford asked the question, "How would you treat a friend who has lied to you as often as your fears have?" Without question, that so-called friend would find no audience with any of us. Yet each of us entertains fears that seek to undermine and destroy.

The Bible says, *"Perfect love casts out fear"* (1 John 4:18). The love of God is so overwhelmingly powerful that nothing in opposition can stand in its way. The love of God brings such a sense of security that faith (trust in God) finds the perfect climate in which to grow. The result? No fear. David put it this way, *"…my heart shall not fear…I will be confident"* (Ps. 27:3).

What is there that is so solid that I can always be confident, no matter how bad I've messed things up? Only the *love* of God. Let's allow Him to conquer our hearts with His love again and again and forever rid us of the terrorist of the soul.

48

CARTOONS

I saw several "Christian cartoons" that made me laugh. One featured the little boy who donated his lunch for Jesus to multiply to feed the multitude. He later came to the disciples asking, "About my loaves and fishes...could I get a receipt for tax purposes?" Then there was the pastor who is enjoying a day at the beach. He picks up a seashell and puts it to his ear and hears a voice, "So you thought you'd get away from the church for a day, huh? Don't you feel guilty? And what about all your parishioners? And you call yourself a pastor..."

One of the funniest was the billboard in front of a church that read, "The Lite Church—24% fewer commitments, home of the 7.5% tithe, 15-minute sermons, and 45-minute worship services. We have only 8 commandments—your choice. We use just 3 spiritual laws and have an 800-year millennium. Everything you've wanted in a church...and less!"

My favorite is perhaps the picture of the pastor who is talking to his wife in the front row of the sanctuary. He says, "My ear kind of hurts." The man behind him turns to his wife and says, "The pastor has an earache." Behind them is a woman who overhears their conversation and turns to her husband, saying, "The pastor's got a hearing aid!" Alarmed, the woman behind them turns to her husband with the news, "The pastor's having trouble hearing!" The teenagers in the back row excitedly turn to one another with a new bit of information, "The pastor got a double earring!" The poor woman walking in the back door overhears the last statement, turns around and leaves the church, muttering, "That does it. I'm out of here."

Laughter really is good medicine. The cartoons I described were taken from *Leadership* magazine and have enough truth in them to be imaginable. Bill Cosby continues to smile all the way to the bank because he knows how to see humor in real life situations. It's a gift from God.

On the other hand, humor was never intended to be at the expense of another person's self-esteem. The idea of a "roast" where people take turns putting someone down in the name of humor is as far removed from the Gospel as is a dirty joke. Human integrity is to be preserved.

But let's face it, life has its funny moments. Lighten up and laugh.

49

TLC Conference

Beni and I attended Iverna Tompkin's TLC week for pastors and their wives.

I have wanted to attend one of Iverna's conferences for a long time. I not only attended, she asked me to teach. What a great honor.

Over the years, we have found it very important to take part in conferences made available for pastors. At times we have also been able to take some of the leaders from the church. These meetings have been a source of great encouragement and instruction for us all.

Iverna's is the most unusual conference that I know of. She only allows twelve couples to attend. She, along with her brother Judson Cornwall and several other "heavy hitters," teach this small group day and night. There are very personal ministry times with the pastor and his wife (one-on-one), and there are times with full-class settings. All in all, it is the most intensive and in-depth ministry time that I have ever heard of for a pastor. To attend is a privilege. To teach is frightening, but also a great honor.

One of my most valuable possessions is people's prayers. Prayer support sometimes means the difference between success and failure. There are no great men and women—there are those whose ministries are bathed in prayer and those whose aren't.

The lasting quality of any ministry depends on the issue of prayer. Please pray for your church staff and families as well as others who fill leadership positions. A pastor's strength is oftentimes your prayers.

Now it came to pass, as He was praying in a certain place, when He ceased, that one of His disciples said to Him, "Lord, teach us to pray, as John also taught his disciples." So He said to them, "When you pray, say: Our Father in heaven, hallowed be Your name. Your kingdom come. Your will be done on earth as it is in heaven. Give us day by day our daily bread (Luke 11:1-3).

50

LESSONS FROM LARRY'S TESTIMONY

I had the joy of listening to Larry Feezor give the testimony of God's work in his life. It was at the Trinity County Christian School chapel service. You see, I was to be the speaker that morning, but felt it would be best if Larry could share what God has done. And so he did.

He spoke some of the past—the drug arrest, the near-fatal logging accident, and the most recent motorcycle accident that took the life of a friend and left him paralyzed from the waist down. While the past was never glorified, it was clear that sin brings pain. The great message of his testimony is twofold. One, God is a God of forgiveness. Even though God had His hand on Larry's life for several years, he had not walked true to God's will for a good part of that time. Yet God forgives and restores. The second part is this: *"God causes all things to work together for good to those who love God, to those who are called according to His purpose"* (Rom. 8:28 NASB). This is the great promise for all of us. It will work for good, because we belong to Him.

Previous to that great promise is the verse that states, *"the Spirit Himself makes intercession for us"* (Rom. 8:26). What a wonderful thought. The Spirit of God is praying for us 24 hours a day—and does He ever know how to pray! Following the declaration that all things work for good is another bit of good news. *"Christ Jesus...also intercedes for us"* (Rom. 8:34 NASB). No wonder all things work for good! Look who is praying for us. Both the Holy Spirit and Jesus are representing us before the Father, and they pray according to the Father's good will.

Like the rest of us, Larry's story is still in the making. He did a great job, and will continue to do so. And like the rest of us, part of the "making" process is found in telling others what God has done. If we wait until we are the finished product, we're finished before we start, but are never complete. Ministry to others brings maturity.

Speak with confidence. Remember, you are *always* being prayed for!

51

Ministry Excuses

One of the greatest responsibilities in my position as pastor is to release people into ministry. In attempting to do this I often get some very interesting responses, some of which I'd like to address.

"I'm not mature enough for that kind of ministry." If any of us are fully qualified for a task in the Kingdom, we'll struggle with the idea of being totally dependent on God. When I first moved to Weaverville to pastor, someone I met in the community said that I was too young for the position. I had to agree, because that's just what I thought. But I came because of God's call.

How old does someone have to be in the Lord before they begin to serve? The same day you're saved. Maturity doesn't launch you into ministry. Ministry launches you into maturity.

"I don't feel that I have the 'gift' needed for that ministry." The main problem that I had with the idea of being a pastor is that I was expected to talk in front of people. That wasn't my nature, or so I thought. Jesus said, *"Give to him who asks you"* (Matt. 5:42). Ministry is not ours to control. It is to happen according to the need. Serve God at every opportunity, and He will enable you.

"I don't have the time." Some of the busiest people I know are the best servants. They know how to live by their priorities. That ability has a powerful effect on their whole life, giving success and achievement.

"The pastor hasn't approved my ministry." Ministry cannot be separated from the normal Christian life. Upon conversion we have God's approval—a pastor's is not needed. Speaking the Gospel, visiting the sick and needy, checking up on someone you haven't seen for a while, taking food to a family in need, studying the Bible with friends, praying for the sick, leading someone to Christ, comforting the discouraged, provoking into action those who tend to be apathetic, ad infinitum—that is the normal Christian life.

If you are called to an ongoing public ministry, for safety's sake, allow others to help you become successful in it. Wolves gather where there are no leaders.

"I'd love to." When a church member was asked to help set up our equipment early Sunday mornings, his response was, "I'd love to! How could I say no to an opportunity to serve?" We all have needs—to serve and to be served. It's not only a great responsibility, it's great fun!

HOUR OF OPPORTUNITY

In the early 1990s, Beni and I attended the District Council meetings for the Assemblies of God. We had a wonderful time. My parents were honored for completing their 10th year of service at the headquarters office. They were given a trip to Hawaii and a sizable financial gift. It was great to see them blessed in this way.

I was asked to sing my song, "Answer by Fire," and teach it to the 2,500+ present. When Bob Kilpatrick heard the song, he wanted to play and sing with us, which topped off the event for me. Bob Kilpatrick, Beni and I sang, and our own Bob Johnson played the piano. Such fun.

After returning late from the Wednesday night meeting, we were appalled by news of the riots in Los Angeles. It was crazy, literally. Like many across the country, we were glued to the news. The week prior, earthquakes. This week, the shaking of the human soul.

There is no permanent answer for events like this apart from Christ. The message we bear is that important.

Over the years the Church has been in the news, and it has not always been good. I believe that God allows situations to come to the forefront that human-kind has no answers for, thus giving the "humbled" church the opportunity to bring a solution.

I remember a case in point: Governor Pete Wilson (governor of California from 1991-1999), was very moved by the challenging message of long-time friend Richard Halverson, Chaplain to the U.S. Senate from 1981-1995, and expressed his desire for the Church to bring the answers to the needs of human-kind. Not only that, the governor also met with Donnie Moore (of the Radical Reality youth ministry team) to see how he helped the youth of our state to get off drugs and return to morality. Our governor took steps to lay out a plan to release the Church into its rightful place of influence.

Pray that we might recognize our hour of opportunity.

53

SELLING THE HOUSE

Beni and I have struggled for quite some time about whether or not we should sell our house. The reason: we have broken some of God's standards regarding debt and have felt its sting. What should have gone to the support of our building, missions, or simply family has been devoted to the "Visa Empire" in the form of finance charges. While we have not been people who go out and buy washers and dryers and the like on credit, we have obtained debt beyond what is wise. The reasons are only excuses.

Three years ago we bought the beautiful home that we now live in. It took a series of miracles for us to buy that house. God was generous as usual, and allowed us to buy it at a time when local home values were about to increase. It was our first home, tucked in the woods, quiet and attractive.

Our struggle in deciding whether or not to sell was not because of our tie to an attractive home. (I've determined not to hold on to "things" tightly.) While we have enjoyed this house immensely, that was not the problem. In thinking about selling, we were concerned about whether or not we were bailing out of a trial before God's intended miracle. But it's sometimes hard to hear God's voice when my own is so loud.

Someone had shown interest in buying our home, but it wasn't listed yet, as we had not determined what the will of God was in the matter. After wise Christian counsel one Friday morning, it became obvious to us that God wanted us to sell. By that afternoon our house was sold.

Then came the arduous task of finding another home. We found one that seemed to be our best option. Our offer was accepted. And we waited (my favorite thing to do) for loan approval, escrows, and anything else that needed to be taken care of before the big event. We were excited about the move (not the moving!) and had no regrets about the decision. It was a new phase in our lives.

Something I've noticed over the years is that when your pastor goes through changes, the church soon goes through the same thing. Because this was such a positive move, I share it with you for your encouragement. It is time to get out of debt if you're not already.

And it is time to devote more of ourselves (time, skills, money, etc.) to the Last Days harvest. You may have already made that commitment. My word to you is that God is making a way!

54

BIRTHDAYS

I give a special birthday gift to my children when they turn 10, 13, 16, 18, and 21. It's a letter. Just a letter from Dad. In it I talk to them about how they are a gift to me and about their gifting from God. Oh, it's probably another sermon (of which they claim to get many), but it is given as an emblem of promotion—acknowledging that they are entering a new level of life. Why those particular years? I don't know. It just seemed right.

Birthdays…the event we longed for as children, and learned to despise or ignore as adults. Why were birthdays important to us as children? Presents certainly played an important part of the celebration. And oh, the parties—our friends could come and play games we'd never play at any other time, cake and ice cream, door prizes—all in our honor. But there was one more aspect that was important to us then. We were older. Do you remember being 10? How about 10 and a half? Why, I think I can even remember being 10 and a quarter. Getting older, growing taller, becoming more independent—all were parts of the youthful passion for birthdays.

Then we get old and grouchy. It doesn't happen at any particular age. In fact, it happens at around 60 for some and around 25 for others. And for a special few, it never happens.

Our culture has lost much of its admiration for age. Youthfulness is sought for and persevered at all costs. What happened to the value of age? With it is to come wisdom, experience, and esteem. Are those values still valuable?

I'm also wondering if the distaste for birthdays is indicative of a lost passion for growth. As children we measured ourselves against the wall, with markings and dates to chart our progress. I remember a time in my walk with the Lord that I was very aware of my growth (to a fault). Is that childishness, or childlikeness?

Perhaps the general dislike for birthdays among adults has nothing to do with the spiritual condition of our day. In fact, my whole question may be the result of my being over-reflective. But just in case, enjoy your birthday and be always growing!

A Welcome Discovery

One year I found that I had an allergy to dairy products. While drinking milk had never been tempting, I do like my ice cream. After suffering with stomach problems for so long, Lactaid, an over-the-counter product, was a welcome discovery. I could eat ice cream, cheese pizza, and all the other things that had been making me sick for years.

On a trip to Africa, I ran out of this much-needed medication. I was especially distressed because I couldn't eat this wonderful dessert called flan, a custard-type dessert with burnt brown sugar on top that is made with milk. Pharmacies there had never heard of such a thing. Tragic. I was soon to go to Paris to meet my wife. Both France and Italy share the role of being the ice cream (gelato) capitals of the world. When I left Africa, I purposed in my heart to find Lactaid in France.

Beni and I went for a romantic walk in Paris, and we found a pharmacy. When we asked for a digestive enzyme specifically for milk they brought out their reference book on medicines. Nothing. A woman customer next to me offered her assistance, saying she was a medical doctor. As it turned out, she was the doctor for the U.S. Embassy in Paris. Not only did she know about Lactaid, she informed me that they didn't have any in all of France. She then reached into her purse, referring to herself as a "fellow sufferer" and handed me her own bottle of Lactaid. She was concerned that this fellow American would be in Paris and not be able to enjoy ice cream. Hallelujah!

I never ceased to be amazed at God's attention to the details of life that have no real significance, except to us. How did I know what pharmacy to go to? Or when to go? I didn't. I didn't hear a voice saying, "Thus saith the Lord, go into that pharmacy and I will provide for you there."

Walking in the Spirit was never intended to be a testimony of our maturity. Instead, it's the ongoing testimony of His faithfulness through fellowship, even when we have no idea what He is doing.

56

ADVERTISING

Years ago we (the church leadership) discussed putting advertisements in the *Trinity Journal* citing our service. I hadn't been too thrilled with the idea, but it seemed like it might be a good thing. The problem I had with it is that when I turn to the religious page of the local newspaper, it looks more like twenty of the same businesses competing for the customer's attention. And competition in the Church always turns my stomach.

Can you imagine what it would be like if we really competed? I can see it now, "Attend Generic Assembly, home of the 6 percent tithe, the fifteen-minute sermon, and the condensed version of the Bible." No thanks.

Besides, I don't think the usual way of church advertising works to reach the unsaved. It only informs the religious community (the only ones who read that page of the paper) what's happening in other churches. Now that you understand my completely unbiased opinion, let me tell you what we decided.

I was commissioned to put some ideas together. I came up with various concepts that we could use:

1. It must promote the Gospel of Jesus Christ above any of our programs, or even Calvary Chapel as a ministry.

2. It is to reach the unsaved. Therefore, the ad should address solutions to human need.

3. Ads should not be preachy or try to give too much information. It is more like a small tract. Remember K.I.S.S.—Keep It Simple, Saint!

4. It must be presented in an attractive way. The way of the King is excellence!

5. There must be no trace of a competitive spirit in the ad. For this reason we end every ad with a message like, "Please visit one of the many fine churches in Weaverville this Sunday."

Then Jesus went about all the cities and villages, teaching in their synagogues, preaching the gospel of the kingdom, and healing every sickness and every disease among the people (Matthew 9:35).

HIS PROBLEM

I returned from the Friday morning prayer meeting to find water bubbling up from the ground in my front yard. Upon further examination, it was apparent that there was a leak in a pipe belonging to the city. Upon even further examination, with my nose, from a distance, it became obvious that it was a sewer pipe.

I quickly went into the house to discover the family already knew there was a problem. They just didn't know that it involved the outside too. Towels were all over the bathroom floor. The shower stall was a small pond. And all my family members had that look that said, "I sure wish I could use the bathroom."

My first thought was to call our plumbing genius. Beni had already done so. He came quickly. After examining our situation for about ten seconds, he called the county saying it looked like their problem.

We had been remodeling for about six weeks, and during that time we had many problems that are typical of such projects. However, this is the first one that belonged to somebody else. What a discovery. It was like finding gold or striking oil. A rare event indeed—someone else's problem.

But come to think of it, all my problems are supposed to belong to Somebody else. I seem to understand and live by that principle for seemingly brief periods of time. Because we live in *His Name*, for *His glory,* we are covered by *His care.* That means that anything that I would naturally be concerned about is something He will supernaturally care for…if I will trust Him.

The next time you have a concern about something, call the Kingdom County Office in prayer and let Jesus know that He has a problem. He's never too busy to take your call.

58

A Time to Sleep

In 1973 I was working in the Salt House (an outreach/discipleship center for youth) in Redding, California. Little did I know that the experience that I had there would mark my life and ministry forever. It seemed that every demon-possessed person on the West Coast would frequent that place. It was "Christian education" at its best.

Some of our experiences are great lessons for life. Others are just funny parts of life. After one of those late nights of ministry, I was sleeping zealously (if that's possible). The phone rang and I answered. I don't know how long I had been on the phone before the realization hit that I was sleeping. Oh, it wasn't a dream. I woke up while talking to someone on the phone. And who knows what I said.

Years later I was counseling a couple in my office. I had spent countless hours with them trying to help heal their marriage. It was a hot summer day, and my office was quite warm. As the gentleman was talking I became very tired and fell asleep. My blinks were getting longer until my eyelids finally stuck together. I didn't sleep long and the guy talking never noticed. But when I woke up it was similar to the feeling you have after nodding off at the wheel of a car—scary, and thankful that nothing happened. He kept talking and I listened with new interest.

The Bible says that sleep is a gift from God. We are also taught that there is a time to sleep and a time to be awake. Peter missed his opportunity for personal breakthrough when he slept instead of responding to God's invitation to *"watch and pray"* (Mark 14:38). As a result, he was tempted and fell.

There is a time to sleep and a time to pray. Do both well and live strong!

59

Summer Camp

"Ready or not, here I come," said the summer to the spring.

"I don't believe it," came the response. "And besides, I'm not ready for you to come. I'm not through with...."

"CRACK!" said the winter, interrupting with what little strength he had left. It was the sound of an earthquake in the air as it repeatedly rattled the windows of the Trinity County residents. Winter never was one to leave quietly, you know. For some strange reason, unknown to even earth's best scientists, winter shows up whenever spring and summer fight. And so the battle continued, with lightning flashing again and again. Thunder echoed through the mountains as spring and summer clashed in battle like two great warriors from the days of armor-clad soldiers. The conflict became fiercer until finally there seemed to be a definite winner.

And so it was that spring gave way to summer, just in time for Calvary Chapel's family camp. The believers rejoiced around their campfires, singing songs, enjoying the fellowship without the distraction of telephones, televisions, and tele-neighbors.

And an amazing thing happened: the food seemed to taste better in the great outdoors; the Scriptures took on new meaning as they were read; and even the children (for generations to come, I'm told) thanked their parents for building such memories with the priority of Christian fellowship.

It has even been said that in the record books (kept only in Heaven, of course), a certain June camping ritual was kept for generations. The cloud of witnesses were so moved by the sight that they requested a holy campground be constructed next to the glassy sea, just to remind them of their heritage. I can't verify this, but it does sound reasonable to me.

History in the making—plan your own today.

60

ERIK AND STEFAN

We first met little Erik and Stefan at family camp. They had come with the Thompsons as the latest guests to their group home. Their smiles were some of the most contagious that we had ever seen. So inviting. One wonders how children of great tragedy could still have such a love for life. The answer can only be God's grace.

For my whole family, it was love at first sight. Immediately Beni talked of adoption, or at least foster care. Her wheels were turning fast, getting all the information that we would need to make an intelligent decision. Many conversations, phone calls, and an application later, we had two new boys in our home. Their ages were four and six. They also had three brothers placed in two other homes. Because of all the stressed packed into their short lives, weekly visits to the counselor were necessary. The smiles that had attracted us to them continued. But we soon discovered tears and pain—the products of their past. Nightmares, behavioral problems out of the ordinary, and graphic descriptions of their past began to pour forth as an unstoppable force. But love does indeed cover a multitude of sin.

We took them on our vacation, celebrated birthdays, enjoyed Thanksgivings and Christmases together. They called us Mommy and Daddy from the beginning (without our prompting). I wish I could say that all the problems that they brought with them are gone. They're not. But the visits to the counselor are no longer needed. The nightmares are gone, as are most of the hellish descriptions of their past. God's grace again shines for children.

This has been a family commitment. Each of us has had to make adjustments—which is kind of like saying the Grand Canyon is a big hole—but God's will is what is important. And that is seldom without cost, and never without reward.

My purpose for writing this is simple. There is a great need for more foster parents. I wanted to give you an invitation to this challenge that was honest. Is it convenient? Never. Easy? No. Worthwhile? Absolutely! We have had the chance to change lives.

Is this for everyone? No.

Please consider.

61

Jamie Buckingham

Jamie Buckingham died. He was a well-known pastor and author. He wrote many books and was the editor of *Charisma* magazine and the "for leadership" counterpart called *Ministries Today*. His candid writings brought much insight and encouragement to the Body of Christ. I, for one, am indebted to him.

His honesty could make me feel nervous. He would deal with any subject, seemingly without fear. Sometimes he seemed harsh, but more for himself than for readers. He caused my heart to weep, my mouth to laugh, and occasionally he even made me angry. But he was always genuine. When my copy of *Charisma* would arrive in the mail, I would almost always turn to his article first. He wasn't a "doom and gloom" prophet. The difficult task of being a realist with hope was one he handled effortlessly.

It feels so strange to write a eulogy for a man I never met. I never even sat under his ministry (though I had hoped to attend his writing seminar). He was a personal treasure. And I miss him.

His final year was his greatest because of what God did *in* him. Through tragedy he was launched into personal revival. Every moment with Jesus and His people, carrying out His will, was precious. He had a sober approach to life that was neither pious nor infertile. He was simply distracted, and rightly so—he had tasted Heaven.

His last article in *Charisma* (February 1992) ended with this prayer:

Lord, keep me aloft without being aloof. Show me how to remain in orbit with you above Earth's poisoned atmosphere, yet dipping at your command to touch, instruct, and heal as Jesus did. May I never be "of this world." May I always—in my own mind and in the oft-critical eyes of others—belong to a different kingdom. May I be in the world but not of the world, ministering at your pleasure, marching ever to the sound of the different drummer.

Thank you, Jamie. You fed me well.

62

THE GREAT HORSE RIDE

Beni and I had dinner with friends who lived on a ranch. They had a couple of horses, one of which liked to run a lot. In fact, they had to keep it in a small corral, or it would run itself to death.

You need to understand, a horseman I am not. But they asked me if I would like to take him for a ride. I don't know if it was ego, a sense of adventure, curiosity, or what, but like a fool I said yes. And what a ride it was. This horse ran like it was on fire. I was beginning to wonder about a lot of things—my sanity being one of them. But honestly, survival was uppermost on my mind.

Horses are usually not too bright. In my situation, the horse was brighter than I was and it knew it. After running at the speed of sound to the other side of the property, it turned around and ran back toward my wife and friends (none of whom, I might add, had the look of intercessors). On the way back, it spotted a tree. This tree had limbs that were slightly higher than the horse's head. This was about to become a disturbing fact.

In a split second, I learned how to melt into horsehide, lie prostrate, and pray, all the while staying attached to the saddle. The branches skimmed over my back, and I brought the horse back to the owners saying something like, "Wow, that was great!" I didn't lie. Remember, "great" was used to describe the earthquake of 1904.

A few days later I heard a good statement that I can't quote verbatim, but will come close. "If you always do things the way you've always done them, you'll always be where you are now." Be open to seasons of change, and be ready. Sometimes life is very similar to my horse ride—wild, scary, and "great"! But all of God's changes have adventure and carry His promise, *"I am with you always"* (Matt. 28:20).

What more could we ask for?

63

NAMES

What's in a name? Whether it's Fred, Walter, Gladys, or Jean, some would say, "A name is just a name." That is, unless you get stuck with one that causes embarrassment. Like the girl named Ima. Her last name was Pigg.

Some names seem to be more dignified than others. Winston Churchill, for example. Can you imagine his name being Bubba? "We'd like to welcome our guest this evening, the honorable Bubba Churchill." It just doesn't sound the same. (No offense, all you Bubbas.)

I remember as a child thinking that people with unusual names became more famous. People with names like Bill Johnson were nonachievers. My world of famous people was filled with professional baseball players. It took me awhile to realize that the reason they had unusual names was because they came from other countries where their names were probably normal, like Felipe Alou and Orlando Cepeda. Don't get me wrong. I wasn't asking for a name change to Felipe Johnson.

Since we put some $30,000 into building a new road to our property, the county has given us the privilege of naming the road. Now you'd think that this would be an easy task. I asked the church members for ideas. Some, being the more spiritual types, wanted names like Repentance Way or The Only Way. One even suggested The Inner Court. I'm sure that others would be blessed to the max with the name Jesus Loves You Road. Some thought using a signpost as a tract is a little excessive; they preferred Glenn Oaks, East Bluff Road, etc.

I tended to stay in the camp that wanted a name that had meaning to us, but wasn't overtly spiritual—like Azusa Street. It's a funny sounding word, but it was the location of one of the greatest revivals of this century. Or how about Oasis Road. Oasis is a good name, referring to a place of refreshing. Another that came to us was Embassy Road. Embassy (not Suites) means a body of persons entrusted with a mission to a government. That's us. People, representing one government, the Kingdom of God, sent to another. Considering our growing place in worldwide ministry, that may have potential. An embassy is also a place of refuge for the citizens it represents, or for others needing their protection. Selah.

And then there are those who liked the more humorous side. One such individual mentioned Not A Through Road. To make it more subdued, I suggested spelling it Naddathru Road. Of course, this generation probably wouldn't appreciate our sense of humor.

It wasn't an easy decision. And just think of poor Adam—he had to name all the animals!

64

Learning from the Experienced

There have been times in my life when God arranged for me to sit under the ministry of one of the generals of His army. They are men or women with far-reaching influence on the Body of Christ. Every time the opportunity comes up, I jump at it. It is awe-inspiring to sit at the feet of those who shape Christian thought for this century. They have spent much time at His feet, and I in turn at theirs.

I always leave those meetings or seminars with a renewed vision of God and His work. But on three occasions I left disappointed—not because the people didn't meet my expectations, but because I saw something in my heart that troubled me. And to be really honest, all three times I saw the same thing.

The first time was a trip to Denver to sit under the ministry of Pastor Cho from South Korea. I caught myself thinking, "When is he going to get to the meat, the profound stuff?" It never happened. I was disappointed that I had heard nothing new, until I realized the problem. I had taught the principles I heard him teach. But he lived them. Because of that, it was more profound than I had eyes to see. For me, I was happy with having correct theology (or perhaps in that stage it should be called "theory").

The second time was when I first attended John Wimber's conference on healing. I went hoping to find a key to the miracle ministry. He taught what I had already come to believe and had taught for the previous couple of years. But the fruit of his ministry was great. Again I realized that I had been satisfied with knowing truth and not living it (in that particular area). The power behind his ministry was that he practiced (put himself at risk for) what he believed.

The third time this happened was at the Kent Henry worship conference in Redding. It was great. But during the meeting I began to see how far I had fallen in this most special area of my life. Much of what he taught (down to the intimate details of scriptural application) I too had taught—around the world. But I had become content with my knowledge of a subject and not with my present experience.

I'll never forget a time when I sat in a room with a group of young men discussing demon possession (only young men can get excited about that subject).

While the conversation wasn't vicious, it was getting heated. Each one had their opinion and expressed it firmly. Finally, a brother spoke up who had dealt with many cases of demon possession as an evangelist in Brazil. He said to everyone, "You don't know what you're talking about. Listen to me, I've dealt with them." And he proceeded to teach us.

I've had people tell me what's wrong with my theology on prayer or other subjects. If they are not known as people who pray much, their opinions matter little to me. I've determined to learn from those who are not just content with good theology, but are people who require the lifestyle or experience to claim true understanding. And I am trying to require that of myself as well.

65

WE ARE ALL ALIKE

Several of my cousins have big brains. In fact, they all have big ones, with some of them carrying gray matter in jumbo sizes. They are lawyers, professors, doctors and the like, and they don't just do their trades—they do them well.

My cousin Paul, a professor of law, appeared on The 700 Club. He was interviewed because of his expertise in family law. It was great to see his insights aired on such a reputable program. Of course, I remind you, he's family. We're not proud, we just rejoice in the truth. (You may ask, "What happened to you?" I don't know. But I think my brain was going to be so big that God thought it best to divide the excess among my relatives.)

The interview came in several different segments. The first three or four times the camera showed him standing in front of his bookshelves. But the last view was of him working at his desk. More than all the wisdom he shared, more than the feeling of "family pride," I will remember his desk. It was messier than mine, which is an achievement, and I was encouraged.

Isn't it strange to see the things that encourage us? For a young person it may come from seeing a fellow student struggle with a particular subject. Some have been edified by hearing me share about going into debt. Still others find solace in the heartfelt confessions of a national Christian leader.

Is this a morbid interest in the weakness of others? I don't think so. We all just like to remember that we're not alone in this world of blemishes and weakness. In case you forgot, we're all alike. And best of all, Jesus got a full taste of our limitations, victoriously!

If, by chance, you find out that my cousin Paul was using someone else's office for his interview, I don't want to know.

66

THE ATTACK GOOSE

I just returned from another enjoyable breakfast fellowship meeting at the golf course. It's quite entertaining. The conversations range from the inspiring story of Helen Keller and the beautiful sign language of the deaf to the hysterical incidents of Bill Derryberry and his "attack goose."

This goose would actually attack him (the owner, the one who feeds it) and anyone else who ventured into what it felt was its domain. The goose also made its own environmental impact—all over the porch. We laughed and laughed.

Then there was the time when the goose actually attacked the car Bill was driving. Not a smart goose! It wasn't hard to figure out why it came to them as a gift. After almost getting killed, finally that encounter had a lasting impact on its life.

We laughed until the tears came. Oh, you would have had to be there—what fun to hear Bill tell the tale.

And now I'm ready for the day. I've prayed and I've laughed and yeah... it is good to regularly fellowship with other believers. Whether you talk about the Bible, serious personal matters, the nation's deficit, the depleted ozone layer, or maybe even a discussion about cholesterol levels, it's good medicine when God's children get together.

*For where two or three are **gathered together** in My name, **I am there** in the midst of them* (Matthew 18:20).

A merry heart** does good, like **medicine (Proverbs 17:22).

No Perfect Churches

Some people feel that if they belong to a good church, or have their children attend a Christian school, there won't be problems—at least not major ones. Nothing could be further from the truth. Problems shape the tender.

Let's consider this Gospel that we are devoted to for a moment: The resurrection came out of the Cross. The power of God for healing came forth because of sickness. The tears of suffering gave place to the spirit of comfort. And according to Scripture, we are not complete without trial and persecution (see James 1:2; 2 Cor. 12:10; 2 Tim. 3:12).

Now, back to our subject. Difficulties come because they are effective in shaping our heart's affections and they give us the opportunity to establish true biblical patterns for life. Does this Gospel work? Apply it to a problem and find out.

People looking for the perfect church live under the constant frustration that unbiblical idealism causes. Can you imagine what would happen if any one of us found and attended such a church? So much for perfection.

This perfectionism is bondage. It's a bondage that leads the critical into legalism and bitterness. Did you know that in Scripture, the critical person criticized in someone else what was wrong in his or her own life? (See Luke 6:42.)

A good church is not one without problems; it is one where the people have a commitment to resolve them in a biblical manner.

The same can be said for Christian schools. Children will have conflict. They will sometimes be rude, jealous, etc. What makes that setting work is the devotion of the school staff to help the students deal with their own attitudes and conflicts in a biblical manner. That's a "real education."

I have to confess that I may have to throw out my theory that there is no perfect church. I recently found a group in our own city who has perfect unity. They have several hundred people in attendance, yet they manage to have true order without bitterness; and believe it or not, without complaint.

But the cost of joining their group is high—they are found in the cemetery.

68

THE BIG GAME

Athletic competition offers great excitement for its fans. It's amazing how a football team can lay their lives on the line for four quarters, only to have the outcome determined by a dropped pass or a field goal with only three seconds to go.

One season, my boys and I watched the final two minutes of two Chicago Bulls games. Both were determined by last-second shots. The players work very hard, sometimes losing over ten pounds in a game, and still it comes down to the final seconds. In one game, the ball was given to Michael Jordan for the final shot. The Bulls won. In the next game, Jordan also had the final shot. He missed, and they lost.

Perhaps my favorite memories come from the now famous Joe Montana "two-minute drill." In those two minutes, each player raised his level of play to an intensity that no one could have for an entire game. The strategy changed from the methodical wearing down of an opponent to a quick strike attack at the "enemy's" greatest weakness by utilizing their greatest strength (much like in combat).

In the 49ers second Super Bowl against the Cincinnati Bengals, we (the 49ers, of course), were behind by a few points with under a minute to go. And then those magic words: "TOUCHDOWN 49ERS!" After two broken legs in that game alone, and who knows how many other injuries, it was won in the final moments.

Behind many of these great victories are coaches and players who rise to the occasion with almost superhuman abilities. In one of the World Series games, the player who dominated the game was a man whose batting average was normally around .250. But that game he hit over .400 in seven games. Why? It was baseball's biggest event.

God's Church may be in the final moments of planning and praying and training. It's time to "arise and build." We must come as the two spies of Israel that Moses sent into the Promised Land, who against all odds said, "God is with us, it can be done."

The thing that excites me most is that some who have a batting average of about .250 are about to enter that realm reserved only for the courageous. The reason? It's the Big Game, and we have the unfair advantage of superhuman abilities.

Or should I say supernatural?

69

WORD FROM MARIO MURILLO

During a Monday night meeting, Mario Murillo prophesied for about ten minutes over our church body. I share that prophecy with you as encouragement and motivation:

You're going to see an intense visitation of God that will begin at the latter part of this summer, and will extend through the entire fall. I'm warning you that it is coming. When it comes, the controversy will surround the intensity of your worship. When that controversy comes, you must not back down. Because, the way that God is going to heal and save this city is through the raising up of Christ—which creates a vertical momentum of exalting the Lord, which will create a vacuum at the bottom. When air rises it sucks in air underneath. As Christ is exalted by the worship of this church, even a level of worship that you've not yet known, it will create a vacuum in the city that will draw people. And you're going to find yourself in the most contradictory position you've ever seen—receiving more criticism and yet seeing more people saved. You'll wonder why so many bad things are being said about you, concurrent with so many people being radically saved. And then the Lord will test the church and say, "Do you want to be popular, or do you want to be effective?"

I ask the same question for you to consider, "Do you want to be popular, or do you want to be effective in the Kingdom of God?"

GOOD COMMUNICATION

Without a doubt, communication is the most addressed problem in the counseling sessions I have had over the years. Unfortunately, it's a skill that we are not born with. This area, when lacking, affects every possible facet of our lives. Communication is something we *must* be growing in as believers.

Some feel that to communicate well they must get across what is on their mind. Paul taught us to "speak the truth in love" (see Eph. 4:15). This requires more than speaking your thoughts. It is concerned with how the other person hears us. In other words, communication is not speaking your mind; it is speaking the other person's language. The overall heart of this as a Christian skill is concern for the other person.

Here are some suggestions for husbands and wives that can help reach the goal of good communication:

- Set your heart on building an "arena of safety." This is a subtle boundary that tells the other person that they are safe with you, regardless of their opinions. Defensiveness is the greatest enemy here. Ask yourself the question: "Do I want to win the battle (argument), or win the war (relationship)?" The natural person has to be right. The spiritual person wants to know right regardless from where it comes.

- Spend time communicating when things are going well. This will give you strength and experience for the more difficult issues. The subjects to be discussed need not be meaningless. They should occasionally be the weightier matters of life like ambitions, feelings, etc.

- Be a listener. This takes time and patience. What makes us good listeners is the excitement we must have for the other person's interests. The heart of the listener is the joy of discovery.

Pride prevents good communication. Love enhances it. Try it. You'll like it.

71

GOOD INTENTIONS

As I glance at my bookcase, I see memories of conferences, bookstores, and other places I've been. Each book stands for an ideal or an area of interest. I like to buy books. In fact, it could be said that I'm a better buyer than I am a reader. Oh, it's not that I don't read, it's just that I buy more than I could ever read in this lifetime.

For example, if I have been thinking about my need to better organize my time, I will probably buy a book on it. I walk into the bookstore, not even intending to buy on that particular subject, and peruse the treasure-filled shelves. My eyes fall upon *How to Become Totally Organized in 15 Minutes,* and I become inspired. A warm feeling fills my heart as I, with honesty, recognize my need. I buy the book and feel good about my commitment to better equip myself for life—and the book sits on the floor next to my desk (which brings up another problem—I tend to buy books and not shelves).

This scenario may be humorous, but all too often it becomes a satire on the rest of life—good intentions without enough power in the intent. Good intentions are sometimes misleading; they can ease the conscience without requiring change and become "clouds without water" (see Jude 12). Many people sit day after day looking at a particular problem in their lives and confess it as wrong. They may buy books, listen to tapes, or even ask for counseling. But the problem remains because there's no action. James said, "I'll show you my faith by what I do" (James 2:18, paraphrase).

Only faith, the kind born in the hours of fellowship with God, can help me rise above the "self help" brand of Christianity into the realm of transformation—metamorphosis! It is faith that joins good intentions with diligence into a marriage that produces change. *"The hand of the diligent will rule"* and *"the soul of the diligent shall be made rich"* (Prov. 12:24; 13:4).

I think I'll go read.

72

RESPONSE TO IMPRESSION CURRICULUM

Years ago, parents from across our state became enraged over the selection of Impression Curriculum for grades 1-6 in many of our public schools. If you are not aware of this material, it is filled with violence and witchcraft. It is not totally corrupt, as there is literature from C.S. Lewis and other great authors, yet the potential for evil is quite sobering.

I have not seen the books firsthand; I have only read quotes from the material printed in *Focus on the Family Citizen*. The following is a small sampling for your examination:

Zini and the Witches—Third Grade Reader

"You deserve to die for this, but I will spare your life on one condition. Bring me the hearts of your mother and sister and you shall live. Not only shall you live, but you shall become one of us. We will turn you into a mighty witch, and you shall help your wife to work evil."

Inside My Feet—Fourth Grade Reader

"The boots kicked and clomped, twisted and turned in mad, frantic frustration, banged me against the fence, until I was bruised and crying for the pain, holding on for life and in despair that there would be no end to the contest until my arms were torn from my body and I was carried off a horrible broken and bleeding stump to greet my mother and father without even the arms to hug them before we were brought to our end."

I met with the parents of a child who has been exposed to the Impressions material. He cannot sleep alone anymore and now cuddles in a blanket at the foot of their bed. Is there any wonder? Why the raping of a child's mind and emotions? All the while, many applaud themselves for their stand against censorship. Thankfully we have many good teachers in our country who would not feed our children with stories like this. But what about those who would? And why was this material chosen in the first place?

This type of curriculum continues to be shoved into classrooms today. What can we do? Frantic quoting of religious slogans accomplishes nothing.

Neither will protest banners or nastily written letters. For the most part, those in decision-making positions want the best for our kids. Appeal to them based on common values. Do your homework, and know what you're talking about. They need our support, and at the same time they need to hear from us.

Don't rise up in uncontrolled anger "in Jesus' name" because we were caught sleeping again. Be involved. Give your input. And remember, many who choose the direction for our schools are elected officials. We elected them.

Go to the polls and let your mind be known.

73

Closet Christians

Everyone from homosexuals to alcoholics seems to be coming out of the closet—even people confessing Christ. Of course, if many of them had been arrested for their faith, they would have been released for the lack of evidence.

Many people consider a "closet" a place to hide so that others will not find out a certain something about them. The Bible looks at a closet in a similar, yet totally different way. The believer is exhorted to go there—not to hide, but to meet with God and to deal with sin. It is there that we come to know Him and are changed into His image. A hiding place? Yes. It's where sin is hidden forever, under the blood of Jesus.

Seldom does a year go by that there is not the news of another Christian leader who has fallen. Exposure of sin in the lives well-known ministers and priests has aroused the awareness of people to the sin that exists in churches. This gives me the opportunity to speak not of them, but of us.

We live in a day when the sin that is not taken to the closet and repented of will be brought into the open. This is God's doing. He is, and always has been, in opposition to sin.

John 4:23 says, "*the hour is coming, and now is, when the true worshipers will worship the Father in spirit and truth; for the Father is seeking such to worship Him.*" One of the ramifications of worshiping in truth is that there is nothing hidden. Honesty to ourselves and to God is the living example of our conversion. Again, this is the nature of the closet experience for the believer. Nothing hidden.

There are actually two kinds of closets. For some it's a place to live because of shame. For others it's the place to go to bury shame. Some go there to hide. Others go there to be exposed. For some their closet is a place of darkness. For others it's a place of light.

The closet, however, is not centered on sin. It is focused on grace. Here we find the key to forgiveness that takes us on to victory. If there is sin, it is dealt with there. But we then move on to faith, courage, strength, and renewed vision. In light of this, let's be closet Christians.

74

ANSWERS AND VETOES

I got to see my heart last night—and it wasn't a pretty sight. Fortunately, this time I saw it before I caused any damage.

Wouldn't you know it, some of God's greatest dealings come to us parents at our children's sporting events. This time it wasn't the umpire, or even a coach who didn't know what he was doing—it was the attitude of certain players and their coaches.

Some consider anger to always be a sin. That idea comes from Eastern religions, not the Gospel. I guess they feel that anger is "bad energy." Jesus taught us that anger is a natural emotion. It's what we do with anger that determines whether or not we have sinned. God's Word says it best: *"Be angry and do not sin"* (Eph. 4:26).

One summer my family and I were vacationing in Santa Cruz. While driving, my children discovered something about their father that they never knew before. He could get angry and yell. An obnoxious driver came within inches of our car and seemed to taunt us with his carelessness over the next 60 seconds. He was right outside my wife's window, so I used her controls and rolled down the window and yelled—no, not profanities. I just asked him, in a rather loud tone, what he thought he was doing. He raised a finger to me to help me understand his feelings for me and continued in his reckless manner.

It's a good thing that when Jesus gave us all power and authority He reserved His right to "line item veto." I can hear Him talking to the Father, saying, "Bill is in a tough situation and he doesn't have a clue what I'm trying to do in him. It would be best if you didn't answer any of his prayers for the next minute or two, or else he's likely to wipe out the entire planet."

Upon my confession, my family was quick to forgive my poor example. It wasn't what I said, it was my heart attitude (the fire in my eyes gave it away).

Last night I yelled at a coach who was swearing at his players. The only thing I lacked was the "cat-o-nine-tails." Speaking out in that situation was not a sin. It's what I thought of afterward that was most ugly. I repented quickly (that is, if you consider about fifteen minutes quickly) and began to pray over the devilish situation. Eventually things returned to a more normal state, and we enjoyed the game of baseball.

So what's the moral of the story (besides the need to overlook my flesh)? Some of the prayers that Jesus doesn't answer enable us to enjoy the ones He does. Be thankful for both the answers and the vetoes.

75

Building Memories

I've always been one to spend money on an object over and above an experience. My reasoning has always been that you have something to show for it after the money is gone. After the special meal, what do you have besides indigestion?

A friend of mine helped me to change my value system to what is probably a more "biblically correct" way of thinking. Experiences are what memories are made of. And building memories is one of the fundamental responsibilities for parents. For a memory to retain its value, it must be creative and enjoyable, but not necessarily expensive.

For me, one of my fondest memories was when I was about 10 years old. My dad took me out of school to go see a couple of Giant baseball games (a favorite pastime). We made the hour and a half drive from our home to Candlestick Park and attended a game. We then stayed in a motel and went to another game the next day. In my growing up years, death wasn't even a very good excuse for missing school. To do so for a baseball game got a "miracle rating" somewhere between the parting of the Red Sea and multiplying the loaves and fishes. This was not only approved of by my parents; it was sponsored by them. And etched forever in my mind is the fact that there is at least one thing more important than school.

Early in our marriage we were really, really broke. We lived in a house that was torn down after we moved out—rent was $95 a month. Our income was from $60 to $100 a week, which was a great increase from the $25 a week that we had started with about a year earlier. We had been using a borrowed car and had just been able to buy an older Volkswagen bug.

Vacation time came and we had nothing. So we took our week and drove to San José to visit my sister and her husband. We didn't have any money to go out for a nice dinner or anything that would seem special to others. Yet we had one of the best vacations we've ever had. We were with friends we loved to be with, who had similar-looking wallets, so we were creative with our time. It remains a treasured memory.

Years ago I attended a funeral of a much-loved mother of six. She was also a grandmother and great-grandmother of many more. While it was a very sad time for the family, the memories that were shared brought joy and life to those burdened with their loss.

We are all builders...builders of memories. Each memory we build stands as a monument to God's grace or our independence. And building by grace is a sound investment.

Remember, the day is coming "When the author walks onto the stage, the play is over"[1] and all opportunity to invest will cease. Build! And by all means, build the memories that testify of His grace.

Endnote

1. C.S. Lewis, *Mere Christianity.*

76

BECOMING GREAT FATHERS

One of the great tragedies of our day is that many men who were not good sons are trying to become good fathers. The attitudes and character traits of a godly child are the ingredients that make us good parents. These truths apply to daughters and mothers too.

While I can't go back and redo my childhood, I can be honest before God about my past and allow Him to restore in me the heart of a godly child.

Too many fail to deal with some of the circumstances that shaped their attitudes and actions at an early age. Honesty is where we must begin. We then follow up on that honesty with an effort to develop godly attitudes and character.

Honesty—be open and transparent before God. Confess what He addresses. Such honesty sometimes requires us to go to those we have offended and apologize. If you owe your father an apology, go to him. If he is dead or can't be reached, confess it all to God as your Father—but by all means do it!

Develop Character—Recognize the place of real character in a person's life. Devote yourself to being a learner of the Christlike lifestyle. Give yourself to the development of godly attitudes.

The following are a few of the traits we were to learn as children: loyalty, honesty, being submissive, respectful, and adventurous. Do those closest to you see these traits in you? If not, find out why and go to God. He heals and restores!

If this were a mere exercise of digging up the past, I could be considered cruel. Rather, it is simply an honest look at how for some the past is very present. Fathers who have the heart of a godly man become great fathers.

Preparing for Fulfilled Promises

During a Sunday morning service, the Lord spoke to my heart about 1985, that it would be a year of "promise." The previous year He gave us a word about 1984 being a year of "double portion." In looking back, I am encouraged by seeing how much God doubled the ministry efforts and blessings.

This word concerning "promise" stirred my heart, because in it I saw how we are to be rooted in the Word of God. The promises of God are not blessings we pull out of a hat. There is an interesting paradox in this subject. On one hand we have promises as a gift of God, something that cannot be earned. On the other hand, they are worked into our lives like polish into a fine piece of furniture, until we are capable of walking in God's provision.

This word from the Lord came at an interesting time for me considering that we were making the first moves toward a building program. We were entering a time when much of what we had seen only in the dreams of our hearts would come to pass.

In considering the days before us I was thinking back to a word given to us in 1981. I searched through my tape collection and listened to the part of the tape that contained this word. To my recollection I have never put a prophetic word in print, perhaps out of a fear that some would think that I considered it equal to the Bible. I don't place any "word" equal to the Bible, but will lay aside my paranoia and print a word that I hope encourages you. The first was a prophetic word, and the second was a prayer that came a day later.

And He told me to pronounce prosperity on this church, because He showed me that ultimately you are going to have a tower up with an FM signal broadcasting gospel music 24 hours a day, and that He is going to raise up people in the body that will be able to underwrite those kinds of projects. He also showed me that you're going to have a resource center and that you're going to get your service and your worship on home video cable and tapes and go around the area here and have home groups where through the television set you're going to have your service recorded and visible to these people. And so the Lord wants the congregation to prosper, not so there will be fat cats, but so that they can get the Gospel out. And the Lord just gave me this word, He is grooming you for generosity. He is conditioning you for prosperity. Praise the Lord!

I pray that in the Name of Jesus Christ you'll open up the windows of Heaven and pour out a blessing that there's not room enough to receive it. Lord, I'm claiming acreage for this church to expand. I'm claiming a new parsonage. I'm claiming a resource center. Lord, we're claiming a tower in which there can be a wattage in this area in which the Gospel can be proclaimed. Lord, we're claiming a Christian cable system that will bring the PTL, the TBN, the CBN and that it will bring local churches. Lord, we're just claiming the media for the Kingdom of God. Hallelujah!

Let there be Christian newspapers and magazines for Northern California. Lord, let there be Christian bookstores. Let there be Christian art forms. I pray that there will be Christian training centers. Lord, we release prosperity as a sign and a wonder. I bind the demon of poverty in the Name of Jesus that's trying to stifle the creativity of the Christians. Lord, I come against the poverty forces trying to suppress Christianity in this area and I bind it in the Name of Jesus, and we cast it out in the Name of the Lord and we release prosperity for these people. Praise the Lord, it's coming!

This was for the benefit of Calvary Chapel, but it can be applied to every church, every ministry, every region, and every state across the nation. Besides having a corporate vision, I know each of us has a dream that God planted in us at birth. Proverbs 20:5 says that this plan is drawn out by understanding, which can come only from the Word of God permeating our minds. So whether it's the dream of the church or your personal dream, next year will be a year of seeing old promises and visions realized.

How can we prepare ourselves for fulfilled promises? It is clear throughout the Bible that we have a responsibility in every promise. I leave you with this verse that we should memorize.

Every place on which the sole of your foot treads, I have given it to you, just as I spoke to Moses...Have I not commanded you? Be strong and courageous! Do not tremble or be dismayed, for the Lord your God is with you wherever you go (Joshua 1:3,9 NASB).

78

STEWARDSHIP

The widow was at her lowest point. She was down to her last meal, and then she and her son would wait until the inevitable happened—death by starvation. God in His mercy sent the help that was so desperately needed. His name was Elijah. He came to her with a word from God. But like much of God's deepest work in our lives, the word didn't have the appearance of the "hand of God."

The direction that God had given Elijah would require him to lay the credibility of his ministry on the line of misunderstanding. He was to ask for her last meal. She was also put into a vulnerable position by having to place complete trust in the word of the Lord (through a fallible man). After Elijah gave his unusual request, he prophesied of God's endless supply, if she was obedient.

If in fact the widow had prayed that God would provide for her, His answer came in a most unique way. It was hidden in a challenge. The first lesson we see here is that things aren't always what they appear to be. God, the One who oversees all the circumstances of my life, often tests my heart to see what, or who, I put my trust in (see Deut. 8:1-5) and as the Scriptures declare, *"He made darkness His secret place"* (Ps. 18:11).

Second, in order to see the miracle dimension of God's provision, the widow had to meet the challenge that meant possible death. This is a level of stewardship that few of us have ever been challenged with. She, in essence, was responsible to initiate the working of the supernatural through obedience.

Third, she still could have starved to death, even after praying for God's provision. Had she failed to meet this challenge, she would have gone the way of many others who were also affected by this drought. To restate it, she would have died because she was unwilling to be generous beyond reason.

These lessons of stewardship affect more than money—they include our hidden talents and desires, gifts for ministry, personalities, physical bodies, and the like. What we are and what we have belong to God. If we pray for the supernatural to be demonstrated in an area of our lives, be ready to meet a challenge beyond reason.

About Bill Johnson

Bill Johnson is a fifth-generation pastor with a rich heritage in the Holy Spirit. Bill and his wife, Beni, serve a growing number of churches through a leadership network that crosses denominational lines and builds relationships. The Johnsons are the senior pastors of Bethel Church in Redding, California. All three of their children and spouses are involved in full-time ministry. They have eight wonderful grandchildren.

Recommended Reading

A Life of Miracles by Bill Johnson

Basic Training for the Prophetic Ministry by Kris Vallotton

Basic Training for the Supernatural Ways of Royalty by Kris Vallotton

Developing a Supernatural Lifestyle by Kris Vallotton

Dreaming With God by Bill Johnson

Face to Face by Bill Johnson

Here Comes Heaven by Bill Johnson and Mike Seth

Hosting the Presence by Bill Johnson

Loving Our Kids On Purpose by Danny Silk

Purity–The New Moral Revolution by Kris Vallotton

Release the Power of Jesus by Bill Johnson

Strengthen Yourself in the Lord by Bill Johnson

The Happy Intercessor by Beni Johnson

The Supernatural Power of a Transformed Mind by Bill Johnson

The Supernatural Ways of Royalty by Kris Vallotton and Bill Johnson

The Ultimate Treasure Hunt by Kevin Dedmon

When Heaven Invades Earth by Bill Johnson